#ME TOO

*Essays About
How and Why This Happened,
What it Means, and How to Make Sure
it Never Happens Again*

Edited by Lori Perkins

For more information contact:
Riverdale Avenue Books
5676 Riverdale Avenue
Riverdale, NY 10471

www.riverdaleavebooks.com

Design by www.formatting4U.com
Cover by Scott Carpenter

Digital ISBN: 978-1-62601-416-9

Print ISBN: 978-1-62601-417-6
First Edition November, 2017

This book is dedicated to

Anita Hill
Tarana Burke
Rose McGowan
And all the women who have come bravely
forward,
and all those who will not be silenced,
and to the next generation
who will not let this happen to them.

Table of Contents

Introduction - Why This Book?

#MeToo—My best friend's niece

#MeToo—A close friend's daughter

#MeToo—My mother's childhood best friend with her own stepfather

#MeToo—Two of my son's close friends

#MeToo—A childhood best friend with a next door neighbor

#MeToo—So many of the women I have worked with in journalism and publishing over the years

The memories of hearing these difficult stories came flooding back to me as I read the *New York Times* and *New Yorker* articles about the sexually abusive behavior of Harvey Weinstein. Then I started to see the stories scream forth on my Facebook feed as Alyssa Milano hash-tagged Rose McGowan's revelation that Weinstein had allegedly raped her, and she had defined her nondisclosure agreement to tell the truth.

And then I remembered that it had happened to me, too.

Not a rape, not even physical sexual harassment, just totally out of place sexual behavior in a work environment.

Lori Perkins

I was the publisher of the local newspaper in Upper Manhattan at 22, but it was my paper that I had started with my own money. I was interviewing one of the middle-aged local New York City politicians for an up-coming election profile, and out of the blue, he asked me if I was interested in being his mistress.

I remember being shocked, and unsure if I had heard him correctly.

He explained that his current mistress was leaving, and he wondered if I was interested.

This was so out of left field that I think I just declined.

Without missing a beat, he then asked if I might want his teenaged children as interns on my paper. He acted like he had just offered me a great job opportunity that I had passed on, but that he was giving me another choice.

I was appalled, but I didn't say anything to anyone, because I think I couldn't believe that we had had that conversation.

At the time, I just assumed that this was the way things were done.

I avoided him after that, and was never alone with him again.

Looking back, I can't believe he propositioned the owner of the local newspaper, and was so caviler about it that it didn't even dawn on him that I might write about it. I also can't believe that I felt it was so normal that I just accepted it, and indeed didn't write about it.

About the same time, my newspaper received a full-page ad from a new bank in the neighborhood, and one of the branch vice presidents requested a lunch with me. I thought it might have been to tell me about a neighborhood program or initiative that the bank was thinking of running.

I didn't remember ever meeting this vice president before, but he must have remembered me from some event, because during the lunch he offered to buy me an apartment.

I told him I already lived in an apartment.

He told me he would buy me one as an investment. It took me about three back-and-forths to realize he was offering to set me up as his mistress.

I made it very clear that I wasn't interested, but never reported the incident to anyone, probably because the paper needed the advertising.

The ad ended up being a one-off.

I am very aware that the situations described above are not sexual abuse, but they are the kind of inappropriate sexual creepiness that men just feel entitled to.

When I told these stories to my grown son, who has always seen me as an empowered feminist mother, he was appalled. "If it happened to you, it's happened to everyone," he said, disgusted.

That's why I put this book together.

We have to tell our stories, point the finger, shame this behavior and make it stop. And if we have to do it every day for the next month, or year, or decade, we have to make that commitment.

The #MeToo movement is part of a larger ripple of change, but most of it has been on social media, which is ephemeral. I wanted to put something together immediately so that we can have a document of this, as a record of the moment in time when we said in unison, "This has to stop."

We are at the tipping point, so let's topple this behavior once and for all.

I hope this book shows the beginning of this particular phase of the movement, one that can be read and passed around as a reference when people look back on this time. The essays range from personal tales and reflection to calls for action and insider stories of abuse in Hollywood. There's also a piece by Alessandra Biaggi about how to get your political mojo on and join the fight.

You'll also see that the tales of sexual predation do not begin with Rose McGowan's allegations of rape, or even Tarana Burke's 10 year-long campaign to support women of color surviving sexual abuse. The first article in this book tells the depressing story of Patricia Douglas, who, in 1937, was the first woman to call out Hollywood's blind eye to sexual assault.

Sexually predatory behavior isn't only found in Hollywood. All we have to do is remember Anita Hill's brave testimony before the all-male Senate Judiciary Committee in 1991, and the fact that Clarence Thomas was, regardless, appointed to the Supreme Court. Stories that exploded after the Weinstein exposé broke included instances of sexual predation among chefs, investment houses, politicians, magazines, newspapers—almost everywhere you turned—because this behavior has run rampant and has been ignored or swept under the rug for far too long.

What started with the early October *New York Times* and *New Yorker* articles about Harvey Weinstein's inappropriate behavior, and blew up into #MeToo, has by now gone global. The hashtag "#MeToo" spread to Sweden, Canada, Norway,

Denmark, Japan, Australia and India, and in France, women have staged their own Twitter revolution with #BalanceTonPorc (squeal on your pigs). The Spanish translation #Yotambién has been trending in Mexico, Spain and South America. In Italy, the hashtag translates into "ThatTime." In Israel, the Hebrew hashtag translates as "UsToo." In Egypt, the Arabic phrase for "MeToo" is trending.

Days of protest, such as the November 12 "Take Back the Workplace" in Hollywood, are happening, and I am sure there will be many more to come.

We know how this laissez-faire attitude towards sexual harassment happened. Now we have to change how we look at the behavior, and make sure that there are consequences. Knowledge is power, and there is strength in numbers: #MeToo has shown us that. We have to tell the stories.

We are not a mob. We are a movement.

We can initiate change by becoming politically active and not waiting for someone else to step up to the plate.

Give money to the organizations and politicians that support the change you want to see.

Back legislation to change the nondisclosure laws in the workplace.

Run for office on the local level, and especially in your industry organizations.

Don't just lean in. Take the reins.

Say something at work, or school, or amongst your friends when you see—or even hear of mistreatment (or give an anonymous tip to HR or the cops).

If you feel you can't do it by yourself, get a group together.

Sign a petition.

Don't live in the "shoulda" shadows anymore.

For me, this book is my way of putting my time and money where my mouth is. I gave up many nights of sleep putting it together, and my staff worked 'round the clock to get it to you in as short a time as possible. The authors donated their pieces for free. Riverdale Avenue Books is offering the ebook for free on all platforms in the hopes that it reaches as many people as possible.

We want to make sure to reach people in the most permanent ways possible. Print is a little more expensive to produce, so we are offering the book at cost (which means we sell it for the cost of printing and distribution, and we take no profit).

So pass this book around. Share it with your sons, brothers, fathers, your daughters, sisters and mothers, your co-workers and friends. Read passages to them, if they won't read it for themselves. Leave it on the desk of someone who should know better. Help us make this movement more than a hashtag.

If you do, we'll do a second and third and fourth edition—until things change.

Lori Perkins
November 2017

Remembering Patricia Douglas, the First Woman to Call Out Hollywood for Sexual Assault

By Raechal Leone Shewfelt

The sheer number of women who have alleged sexual misconduct, from harassment to rape, against once-powerful producer Harvey Weinstein, is shocking. In voicing their support for the victims, many celebrities have indicated that they had had an inkling something was going on, but they hadn't spoken out, frequently saying that they had remained silent because the offending action hadn't happened to them or they didn't want their career to be affected. In other words, over the course of decades, the industry has seemingly accepted such misbehavior as part of show business.

Actress Zoe Kazan made a powerful reference to this in a string of posts on Twitter: "In all the discussion re: Weinstein, not seeing enough about *how* & *why* a predator can fly under the radar in an industry for so long. Sexual harassment being rampant in our industry—being the undertow, the room tone—provides camouflage for the worst kinds of behavior. He may be a monster but he's not a 'lone wolf.' There's a whole system that enables, tacitly endorses & disguises his behavior as acceptable. I hope holding him accountable brings about change. But that only happens if we don't act like he's the exception, when he's an exemplar."

In fact, the woman who seems to have been the first to publicly call out the studios, Patricia Douglas, did so in 1937. Douglas wasn't a famous actress; her IMDb page lists only two uncredited roles as a dancer. But she's noteworthy because of her case, which writer David Stenn documented in the 2007 film *Girl 27*.

"I think she wouldn't be surprised about the allegations [coming out today], and I think she would be modest about being the pioneer in this field," Stenn tells Yahoo Entertainment. "I don't think she ever saw herself as special or unique, and she was both."

The story goes like this: 20-year-old Douglas, who treated acting like a hobby, went to an MGM casting call that she thought was for background work in a movie, according to the Hollywood history podcast *You Must Remember This*. The 120 women who showed up for the "audition" were fancied up and given a skimpy outfit, then taken to a boozy party that the studio was throwing for its executives and 300 salesman to celebrate a banner year. They were the hired eye candy, although they reportedly weren't told anything.

"They never mentioned it was for a party. Ever. I wouldn't have gone!" Douglas, who died in November 2003, recalled to Stenn in an April 2003 piece for *Vanity Fair*. "Oh God, oh God, I wouldn't have gone."

In addition to the women, who were paid $7.50 for their work, the party featured 500 cases of Scotch and champagne. Stenn cited testimony from a waiter at the party saying that the men were drunk and rowdy. The waiter said that he saw "girls get up and move from the tables because the men were attempting to molest them."

Douglas told Stenn that David Ross, from the Chicago office, had tried to "cop a feel" on her during a dance. She attempted to escape into the restroom, but when she came out, she said, Ross and an accomplice held her down and poured liquor into her mouth. She managed to get away eventually, but she said he found her again and threw her into a car, where he raped her.

"When Ross was finished, Douglas stumbled out of the car screaming," *You Must Remember This* host Karina Longworth noted in a 2015 episode on MGM. "[Douglas] was taken to the Culver City Hospital, which, like the Culver City Police Department, was essentially a satellite of MGM. The doctor who examined Douglas said he could find no evidence of intercourse, and Douglas was taken home in an MGM car."

Douglas recalled the trip to the hospital to Stenn in the 2003 story.

"I was given a cold-water douche," she said. "Then the doctor examined me. It's no surprise he didn't find anything. The douche had removed all evidence."

She slept for 14 hours. "I was so sore down there, and my face was still swollen," Douglas said. She didn't go to another doctor, she explained, because she "would've been too embarrassed. Someone would've seen me naked."

Instead, the actress filed a complaint against Ross with the Los Angeles County district attorney, who happened to have a close relationship with MGM studio head Louis B. Mayer. She also tried telling her story to the media, but they would only name Douglas—the *Los Angeles Examiner* published her address—and not the name of the powerful studio, although there was a statement. "We have read with astonishment the alleged charges of the girl," the unnamed studio said. "It is difficult to make any real comment as to a situation which appears so impossible and as to which we know nothing."

The late screenwriter B.P. Schulberg, whose father was once a Mayer partner, told Stenn, "The power MGM had is unimaginable today. They owned everyone—the D.A., the L.A.P.D. They ran this place."

MGM fixer Eddie Mannix did his best to quiet Douglas. It was his job to maintain the studio's wholesome, family-friendly reputation, and he reportedly looked into Douglas's background in an unsuccessful attempt to find something that would discredit her. He even urged other women hired for the party to say that Douglas had drunk too much, although she didn't drink at all. The smear campaign included trying to get Douglas's urologist to say that she'd had a "genital urinary infection"—a euphemism for gonorrhea, Stenn wrote.

At some point, the district attorney did show Douglas photos of men from the party, and she was able to identify Ross. He denied the charges, but the publicity of the case meant that, as Stenn wrote, the DA was "left with no choice but to convene a grand jury." Ross clearly had the advantage, however; he was repped by Mayer's high-powered personal attorney, and because of pressure from the studio, only two of the dancers at the party testified on her behalf. Stenn reported that he had contacted the family of one of the people who had testified against Douglas on June 16, 1937, who said their late relative had been offered any job he wanted at the studio in exchange for silence. Not surprisingly, the hearing did not go the way Douglas wanted.

Douglas then filed a civil suit against several MGM execs and "John Doe One To Fifty" in Los Angeles County, Stenn wrote, seeking $500,000 for their "unlawful conspiracy to defile, debauch, and seduce" the women at the party "for the immoral and sensual gratification of male guests." The studio reportedly kept the case out of court for a while, and then a judge dismissed it. Douglas tried filing a lawsuit in federal court, but her lawyer didn't show up on her court date—suspected to be for political reasons—and neither did the bigwigs from MGM, and that case was also dismissed. Still, it was significant, because the case was "an apparent legal first," Stenn wrote, in that "a female plaintiff made rape a federal case, based on its violation of her civil rights."

When Stenn wrote the *Vanity Fair* story, Douglas was 86. He described her as "a great-grandmother, housebound by glaucoma, emphysema, and fear." And she was still very upset about what had happened to her, so much so that she never talked about it with anyone, not even her family.

"It ruined my life. It absolutely ruined my life," Douglas told Stenn. "They put me through such misery. It took away all my confidence."

For a while after the ordeal, Douglas said, she "went from 'Little Miss Innocent' to a tramp. I did it to demean myself. I was worthless, a 'fallen woman.'"

She was professionally ruined, and what happened in her personal life was worse.

"I've never been in love," said Douglas, who married three times in five years and relocated first to Bakersfield, Calif., and then to Las Vegas. "And I've never had an orgasm. I was frigid." She described herself as "a lousy mother" and "a walking zombie who glided through life."

When Douglas spoke to Stenn, she told him that she was willing to go public (again) all those years later because of her age.

"When I die, the truth dies with me, and that means those bastards win," she said.

Not today.

Raechal Leone Shewfelt is a senior editor at Yahoo News, covering celebrities and pop culture. An L.A. editor since 2009, Raechal is obsessed with '80s teen idols and romantic comedies. She was understandably delighted when "Something's Gotta Give" star Diane Keaton said to her, "You're sweet, but you're insane, OK?"

After #MeToo
By A M Carley

A Puzzler

Did you ever hear the one about the car crash?

A middle-aged man and his son are in a terrible car accident and are rushed to the hospital. The father dies in the ambulance, but the son is still alive when they reach the Emergency Room. Within minutes, a gray-haired surgeon steps in to operate. Upon seeing the young boy, however, the surgeon says, "I can't operate—this is my son!"

How can we explain this sequence of events?

When this puzzler was written, we assumed that boys didn't have a) a mom who was a surgeon, or b) two dads.

And everyone's blind spot to those possibilities was why the puzzler worked. I fell for it too, when I was a kid. Even then, I was disappointed in myself for not considering that the gray-haired surgeon was the boy's mother. I knew that I knew better, but the puzzler did its job. (The two-dads explanation wouldn't emerge until later.)

At least those days are over now, anyway. Right?

Nope. Recent testing in a psychology lab at Boston University showed that even educated daughters of female physicians were stumped much of the time. To be fair, the riddle's language sets up powerful unconscious biases that suggest to the listener a male-dominated scene. The rest, though, reflects our culture's sexism that favors men—especially white, heterosexual men who were born here—and affords them privileges the rest of us dream of and/or resent.

#MeToo

The #MeToo social media hashtag, first coined more than ten years ago by Tarana Burke, exploded in October 2017, after a boost from Alyssa Milano, in the wake of Harvey Weinstein's fall. Its popularity demonstrates that lots of women—and some men— have experienced sexual harassment or assault, and are prepared to go public about it.

Anyone who says they had no idea this was happening has been studiously, astoundingly, willfully oblivious. I mean, we've been falling for that puzzler for decades. We thought James Bond was cool, and, more recently, Don Draper. And last November, in case we needed a reminder, we learned that the office of the President of the United States was going to be occupied by a thug and sexual predator. Tell me again about all that progress we have made; all those hearts and minds feminism has won over?

Serious Questions

How can this surprise anyone? Who can honestly say they were not aware that a powerful bathrobe-clad Hollywood creep could intimidate a woman to the point that she feared for her future livelihood if she did not comply? And how is #MeToo news? Who was not aware that throughout these United States men are harassing and assaulting girls and women every day?

Shame on Me

I began to notice my own response to the viral #MeToo hashtag. I did not want to add my name to the long list of people now going public about their past injuries. Why? I might as well get this one out of the way: Like it or not, I still felt shame. Totally irrational, OK. But over the years, I had asked myself, when things went bad,

- *Had I been responsible?*
- *Did I let those things happen, or even bring them on myself?*
- *Were all those men and boys intentionally evil, or were they just the unaware products of their environment?*

This inquiry is a bottomless rabbit hole. I went looking for sturdier ground.

Shame on Them

I also sensed an implied presumption/wish that if enough of us told the world that sexual assaults and harassment happened, some of the perpetrators would be impressed enough to have a change of heart. In other words, societal pressure could shame the bad guys into mending their ways.

Who really believes that public shaming will solve this huge problem? Show of hands? Anyone? *Bueller*?

Guilt

Or maybe if enough of us speak up and say #MeToo, the "good guys" will recognize the magnitude of the situation and, guiltily, become more active in their own lives supporting feminism and equality. OK. That could happen. And if so, it'll be lovely. Is it sufficient? Nope. Relying on good guys to get us all out of this mess? Really? How has that worked for us so far?

Public Vulnerability

I realized part of my reluctance to say #MeToo came from a concern about the policy implications. I wanted more clarity first, as to what the purpose of all this sharing could be. What could we hope to accomplish collectively? Then I began to worry. Maybe #MeToo is not strategically sound. Might it inadvertently dilute the significance of each of those acts of disclosure? Might sleazy defense attorneys reverse the meaning of the #MeToo groundswell to benefit their clients? It's been suggested that by pumping up the volume of #MeToo's we diminish the heinousness of the acts we refer to. It might look like this:

"But, Your Honor, my client hasn't done anything out of the ordinary—why, just look at all the #MeToo's. This so-called offense isn't rare. All those #MeToo women went ahead with their lives without taking anyone to court. The accuser is just doing this to settle a grudge/gain attention/take advantage of my client's deep pockets. Why should my client be singled out?"

Clearly, we women still need to change our environment. Do we do that by exposing more of our secrets, more of our pain?

Fine Reasons

There are fine reasons to say #MeToo. Many people I respect have done so. Saying #MeToo supports others who need the courage to come forward. The great chorus of voices can help banish undeserved shame, fear, and isolation that many have lived with for too long. The sense of belonging to a tribe can benefit us here. Everyone who knows the truth of sexual assaults and harassment is, in a sense, a member of a club. It used to be a secret society, and it's beginning to throw aside the curtains to let in the light of day.

But is there a reason one more woman needs to educate anyone that hatred and violence against women exist? Part of me gets angry just considering the possibility that any more education could possibly be needed.

Predator in Chief

Especially given that our 45th president revealed himself to be a predator during the debates a year ago, and still got elected—with votes from women—there's been plenty of chatter lately about how wedded we are to our opinions and beliefs. We're not rational about them. We're inflexible. This is why having a calm, fact-based discussion isn't often effective at changing anyone's mind. Our emotions don't reside there.

Belonging Is Stronger than Policy

News items in the aftermath of Charlottesville, Virginia's summer of Nazi and white supremacist invasions indicate that the right-wing hate groups responsible are mostly populated by young men who grew up in environments of abuse and neglect. Then,

Lori Perkins

they are welcomed into a family-like unit and gain the
sense of belonging they've been starved for all along.
They're wired now to be loyal to their new, better
"family" of fellow haters. Their identity, however, is
rooted less in ideology and more in belonging to a
tribe. That's a great example of why arguing about the
issues is likely to be a losing proposition. The issues
are only a veneer. It's not about the issues. It's about
loyalty and belonging, which run much, much deeper
than policy or politics. It's also reactionary: The
backward-facing rhetoric of these groups includes
phrases like "taking back a way of life," "returning to
our values," "preserving white culture," and so on.

Mourning the Mad Men

Isn't it the same kind of deal with men, these days?
Its common knowledge that white masculinity is
threatened, and the white men's hegemony with it. The
Mad Men era, like the Confederacy, has ended.
Weinstein's initial comments justifying his behavior to
the media relied on a version of this argument, in fact.
The poor fellas. The rules began to change without their
permission, and despite their opposition. How can they
be blamed? Oh, darn!

This alteration in the status quo is apparently such a
blow to their sense of well-being that they require an
"other" to absorb their frustration and disorientation.
Who easier than half of the entire population? We're easy
to find. Always have been. Lost James Bond wannabes
mooning for the return of the 60's and 70's that taught
Weinstein so well can pine all they want for the good ol'
days when girls were girls and men were men. There's
no discussing the issues with these people, any more than

with the young Nazis. Their loyalties may be different, but they seem to be just as intractable.

Wait, There's More

I'm convinced that Stockholm Syndrome helped elect 45. Exit polls last November indicated that a boatload of conservative white middle-class women voted Republican. *Even for that guy.* I'm not too confident that these voters, although they now may feel remorse, will be able to step up en masse and recant. They took on the views of their oppressors long ago. Now, like the rest of us, they're wedded to their story, and recalcitrant about ceding any ground.

After #MeToo

There's no need to document any further the existence of sexism and male privilege in our lives. It's pervasive. What we need now is to blow out the remaining parts of the systems that perpetuate it. How? I like to think there are a few things we can do.

Promote Girl Power

If we can't argue fairness or realism or progressive social policy or ethical behavior or justice, what can we do? We can build a better future. A future in which five-year-old girls, and boys, can recognize when physical contact feels unwelcome to them, give voice to their objection, and be supported for it.

A future in which ten-year-old girls can form independent opinions about the world around them— exploring history, economics, music, math, philosophy, writing, building, science, art, social policy, friendship. A future in which they can give voice to their thoughts, develop their skills—including physical skills—and be respected for them.

A future in which 18-year-old young women can cast their first votes based on their own values and their own research. A future in which, if a boy or man (or Stockholm Syndrome-afflicted woman) tries to influence any of those girls at any of those moments, the girls can shrug, perhaps scoff, calmly walk away, and move along, unfazed.

Trust Community and Therapy

Many trauma survivors have emerged from their injuries because of the care and support that they receive from others. In community, our stories can be shared.

In addition, therapy retroactively can repair some or all of the injury for at least some trauma survivors. So those of us who came of age in the pervasive culture of sexism, only to meet its violent manifestations in alleyways, offices, cars, hotels, and everywhere else imaginable, may still sustain hope. Freedom from the internalized ghosts of that dying culture may still be attainable for us.

Mobilize

We are enough.
Each of us is enough.
Collectively we are enough.

Do What You Do Well

Whether that's organizing a march on Washington, a postcard-writing campaign, or a fundraiser, go with your strengths. If your talents are in the arts, go out to the barn and put on a show, make a mural, or draft a manifesto. You get the idea. And if you've got the makings of a politician, see below.

Vote the Rascals Out

It goes without saying that each of us has a responsibility to vote for viable candidates, and, wherever possible, to provide additional support—through volunteering, lobbying, and contributing—to candidates campaigning for women's rights. We can show up at the seats of government and influence the agenda in every way possible.

Just as we can't assume young thugs will change their ways, neither can we assume that the politicians responsible for permitting and/or supporting the systematic destruction of this country's hard-won egalitarian policies will change theirs. Those of us who are able should seriously consider running for office, and the sooner the better. As for the elected officials on the side of the angels, they are straining to defend us against incessant barrages from the Right. They need our support.

Laugh Bombs

One of the seemingly good guys, Tom Hanks, suggests maintaining a sense of humor, too. "'It might be the only ammunition that is left, in order to bring down tyrants," he says. "You know what Mark Twain says: Against the assault of laughter, nothing can stand."

Thoughts and Prayers

A quiet reminder: Don't wait around for any #IBelieveYou hashtags from the good guys in your life. Men's understanding, their empathy, and their thoughts and prayers might be lovely, and are also insufficient. If you have access to them and they help you move ahead, great. If they aren't available, look to your existing community for the support you require. You already know this shit is real. You don't require the validation of the good guys in your life.

What if the girls of the future make up a puzzler to replace the one about the car crash and the surgeon—one that exploits a newly emerged cultural blind spot: an inability to discriminate based on sex?

Here's to laugh-bombing all those tyrants into oblivion. We have work to do.

A M Carley is a writer based in Charlottesville, VA. Her company, **Chenille Books,** provides creative coaching and manuscript development for nonfiction authors. Anne's writer's handbook**, FLOAT: Becoming Unstuck for Writers**, will be joined in late 2017 by an accompanying deck of **FLOAT Cards for Writers**.

The Bully Culture of the Weinsteins
By Jesse Berdinka

A few years ago I read an interesting *New York Times* article about Jeff Bezos, Amazon and the culture of working at the tech giant. What struck me most wasn't the stories of 80-100 hour work weeks, employees pitted against one another, abusive supervisors and people crying at their desks. I had seen similar things (and much worse) in my time as a development exec at Miramax from 1996—2002 working for Harvey and Bob Weinstein.

No—the thing that really jumped out at me were the comments.

One common theme seemed to echo through a lot of them; the claims made about Amazon's culture couldn't possibly be true, because logic would dictate people that smart and capable would surely have enough self-respect and worth to just walk away if they were indeed subjected to the kinds of abuse that people were alleging.

I would love to think that were true.

However, for anyone like myself who ever worked for Harvey or Bob Weinstein, the sentiments expressed in that article were all too familiar. Smart, driven people who want to prove themselves will often seek out the most challenging, even abusive, experiences to prove to themselves and others they have what it takes to be the best—like some corporate version of *Naked and Afraid.* However, *Naked and Afraid* only lasts 28 days, and its physical and mental tests are nothing that sleep and a few good meals can't quickly cure. For many of us, the recovery from working with the brothers was a slower and more painful process.

In retrospect, I think my background set me up perfectly to allow myself to be pulled into this type of work environment. I never intended to work in film. I was a kid from a single mother home who grew up on food stamps and welfare. It was always made clear to me both directly and subtlety that I had a *place.* That people had low expectations for me, or rather the place I had in the dynamic of my small town. So I made a promise to get as far away from rural Delaware as possible, and make something of myself in New York. I finished a stint in the Marines, and moved to Manhattan to work at Valiant Comics as a writer and editor. I have loved comics my whole life, and while I was a horrible writer, I found I did have a knack for story. I was really good at helping other people find ways to express themselves. Both the Marines and comics were amazing experiences for me. The Marines showed me that you could be aggressive and blunt, but still care for people in your charge. Working at Valiant showed me the power of family, creativity and some amazing bosses all working together for a common goal.

I would have stayed in comics, but the speculator crash in the mid 1990's crushed those dreams. I found myself without a job until a friend got me a gig at a temp agency. I did a number of different things, but one of my longest temp jobs was at Miramax in the exhibitor relations department. I would spend most of my days calling theaters to find out if we could send them more *Supercop* Frisbees, or to make sure they were attaching Miramax trailers to whatever big film was coming out that weekend.

It wasn't a glamorous job. In fact, it was pretty bad. I got an ear infection from my headset, and the office was an old warehouse that was cold as hell. The Miramax offices were actually split between a lot of different buildings. Our building handled the un-sexy stuff. The real magic happened over in 375 Greenwich Street—where the development and production execs were. It was only two blocks away—it might as well have been on the other side of the moon. I would look for excuses to take interoffice mail over to the executive floor, but never got past the receptionist. The work was hard, but I was insulated from all of the real craziness. I was happy to even be in the film industry, but still I wanted to be over "there" working on amazing films and collaborating with talented people. I wanted to tell stories.

It wasn't a glamour thing.

I never got caught up in wanting to be part of the red carpet. What really struck me was the culture of people constantly trying to be the best at something, trying to prove something. That resonated with me. From that moment on, I was a willing participant in my own abuse, because I didn't see it as abuse. I saw it as like-minded people working to show the world what we could do.

I got closer when a full time assistant job opened up for the head of Business and Legal Affairs, a lawyer named John Logigian. John was, and remains to this day, one of the best bosses I ever had. He was smart and savvy, and still managed to strike a work/life balance I never saw anyone else achieve. He was one of the few people I ever saw who never let the stress get to him. None of it seemed to faze him. I learned so much about the business and how deals were made. I still use things he taught me almost every day—about business, about people and most importantly about being a father.

John left after a year, and I had spent a great deal of time after work reading scripts and writing analysis of them. I was lucky enough to get a junior development job working on the Dimension side of the company, making genre films. As a kid who grew up watching Universal monster movies on the couch with his grandmother, it was a dream come true.

And that is one thing that all the stories I'm reading about working for the Weinsteins just don't seem to get. The general narrative is that the brothers were indicative of Hollywood hubris and excess—that Harvey (and to a lesser extent Bob) somehow represented the film industry.

Nothing could be further from the truth.

Even in those days at the height of their power, even with all the awards and fame and influence, Harvey and Bob never saw themselves as Hollywood. They were always two kids from Queens fighting and besting a system that didn't think they were good enough to let in. And that "chip on the shoulder" attitude permeated all the way down the chain, through people like me, and all the way to the interns.

That's a very powerful thing. Who wouldn't want to be part of that? When you talk about bullying or abuse, no one ever tells you how to handle it when you identify with the bully. There were times when I felt my attitude of being an outsider, a misfit, a challenger were better understood by people who worked for the brothers than they were by friends and even loved ones.

Many of the film execs in LA where most of the industry happens were hip and fashionable. Many went to fancy schools or came from privileged backgrounds and drove nice cars. None of that mattered when you worked for Harvey and Bob in New York. You could be a middle school dropout as long as you were smart, could do the work and keep up. Sure there were Harvard grads, but there was just as likely someone who never graduated college. In fact, people who came to work from other film companies often flamed out. The culture was just too difficult for them to wrap their heads around—unless you came up in it. Many, if not most of the execs, were former assistants who had toughed it out and earned a chance to do something more. It was an insanely incestuous meritocracy. Still, the opportunities were amazing, if you worked hard.

In two years I went from talking to projectionists about trailers in Des Moines to working with Jay-Z. There was no other place that could have happened.

Those times could be really good. The sheer breadth of talent we worked with was a once in a lifetime experience. I grew up on Hip-Hop and I got to make a movie with Jay-Z and Damon Dash. I loved comics and got to be the point person for our deal with Marvel. Beyond that I had long talks about craft with Guillermo Del Toro and Scott Derrickson. I met

Aaliyah and Stan Lee…on the same day! I spent long days in a room with Charles Stone laughing and working on the script for *Paid in Full.*

That part of the job was fun and rewarding and I loved it, but the other side was dark and increasingly ugly.

As a child who grew up with nothing and constantly had to prove myself to people who didn't think I was worthy, seeing these two brothers stick it to an industry that underestimated them resonated with me. It was my own personal revenge proxy. I love Steven Spielberg. I think *Saving Private Ryan* is a better film, but I still celebrated the Oscar for *Shakespeare in Love* just as much as anyone else because of what it represented, not only to a company where many talented people worked their asses off to make it happen, but also to me personally. I took that victory to heart, and I can assure you I wasn't alone. That feeling of belonging and working for something, of sharing that experience, fooled me into thinking the lows were just the price I paid for belonging.

The problem is you can't be the outsider forever. At some point you have to find something to be *for* instead of *against.* Scrappiness often turns into ego. Ego turns into anger. The culture was one where you had to make a choice. You could become a bully, and there were a few people who chose to do so. You could be an island of calm and protection like my old boss John Logigian, but those people often moved on. You could put your head down, tie yourself to the mast and hope to not be emotionally or intellectually humiliated, or, finally, you could cope with the horror with humor or drink, or whatever else helped you make it through the day.

Personally, I drank and medicated myself—a lot. It's a cowardly but numbing coping mechanism. Many of us younger employees would work from 8:00 to 8:00, if not later, and then go out until all hours—then roll around and do it all again the next day. Days on the calendar had no traditional meanings.

I will be the first to admit that I was weak at times, and resorted to the same horrible tactics as others in an effort to fit in. I once admonished an assistant for not understanding the quality difference between Lipton and Knorr soup mixes—*dry soup mixes*! I'm grateful that he's forgiven me, but I'm still embarrassed by it, among other things.

The abuse was brutal. There is no other way to say it.

I know everyone wants to know the juicy details. I won't go into specifics. No good will come out of it, and in the end it doesn't really matter. Suffice to say that even when you weren't in their presence, the thought of the brothers permeated every moment of working there. I used to tell friends that working for Miramax was like nervously telling people that you "fell down the stairs" when someone asked you where the bruises came from. We all lived for their trips to LA, because it meant five glorious hours of air travel where there was no possible way for them to get a hold of anyone at the office.

Slowly, you start to realize that there is no level that you can get to at the company where it will stop. There is no title, no project you bring in, no work you will do where you can guarantee that you're safe, that the stress will stop.

You start to realize that the things you are really

getting out of it start to become fewer and farther between.

But by then you are stuck, and it's difficult to get off the ride because if you do, then you've basically admitted you can't take it, that you are weak, that everything you might have secretly believed about yourself or been told, about not being good enough, just might be true.

The sick part is, you wanted to be in their spotlight. If you weren't, the shadow could be cold. Your projects might languish, or another exec might be in favor. So even if you hated the experience, you needed to have face time in order to have any type of stature in the company.

If you were just being screamed at it would be bad enough, but the real emotional roller coaster was: you would be a genius one day and an absolute idiot the next. People want to hear about the thrown phones or the screaming. Those things almost seemed comical when they were happening. They were so surreal you almost couldn't take it seriously. The real power of abuse isn't the big things. It's the subtle drip. The slow wearing down of a person by small comments, looks or actions. It wears on you, day after day, sand blown hard against even the hardest of rock. I coped with Xanax and alcohol and a constant gallows humor. Some people rose to the occasion and could be heroic, some did not and became mini versions of the brothers.

It was very clear there was no fighting back. One time a co-worker came to me crying because a high-level exec screamed and humiliated her at a party. I called Human Resources to report it. The result? I was told to watch myself in the hallways because the exec had just taken boxing classes and wanted to make an example of me.

I understand why there are those who can't understand how some of the horrible things alleged to have happened could have, and yet no one seemed to know. I can only say that in the six years I spent there I saw some absolutely reprehensible human behavior, but nothing that was technically illegal or rose to the level they are being accused of. That doesn't mean what went on is even remotely acceptable.

And that's the part that really makes me mad. Rape and sexual assault allegations are serious. I feel for every victim. However, is that the bar we are setting as unacceptable? What about all the horrible things people do to each other every day that we shrug off because they aren't crimes? I know there's a line, and smarter people than me will have to decide where that is.

Harvey and Bob, for all those who suffered nightmares for years, who don't trust anyone anymore because of the way they were treated, who abandoned a career they loved because it became tainted, I have to ask: Is it that hard to be a reasonably decent person? Is the fact that you technically haven't committed a crime enough of a description? What about the way you treat another human being?

There will be those who will read this and say I'm weak or couldn't take it. They are probably right. I tend to wear my heart on my sleeve, and I know I could be a little tougher. I am a person who wants everyone to like him, and I handle politics very badly. But there also came a point where I had to make a decision on who I wanted to be, and the example that Harvey and Bob set wasn't it.

I still keep in touch with many people I worked with. Even before all of this we were a very tight knit and private group. Many have left the industry entirely. Like me, they've become dads or moms and work all over the world doing things big and small. But the thing I think that gives me the most solace and even some hope is that to a person, almost everyone one of them, despite everything, is at heart a decent person.

And I think I speak for everyone I worked with in those days when I say to those working at Amazon or Uber or any place where you are working under unkind circumstances, or worse, under the illusion that at some point it pays off and becomes magical—it doesn't. At some point you will have to decide what type of person you want to be, how you want to treat others—what you *value*.

I hope the value you choose is kindness.

Jesse Berdinka is Chief Creative Officer for Brick Simple where he oversees creative direction for both the company and many of its projects. Jesse has spent over 25 years in storytelling in a wide variety of industries including print, television, film and web. He initially worked in comics as a writer and editor before moving to Miramax Films. While there, he worked as a development exec for such clients as The Onion, Jay-Z and Marvel.

Jesse attended the University of Delaware for History and Political Science. He is a graduate of the Marine Corps Officer Candidate School in Quantico, Virginia and was also a Gunnery Sergeant in the United States Marine Corps. He is an avid reader, and was the 2016 Moth Grand Slam Storytelling champion.

The Big Ugly
By Paul M. Sammon

The recent justified public outing of/outrage over ex-Miramax mogul Harvey Weinstein's sexual predation of countless Hollywood actresses, struggling or established, is a good thing: Weinstein's behavior has been ugly, sordid, and, to its unwilling targets, traumatic. Unfortunately, such abuse of power—and trying to force someone into unwanted physical intimacy - is, in Hollywood, definitely a manifestation of power. It is neither an isolated case, nor a new one. This type of coercive behavior was and continues to be endemic in the entertainment business - long before the term "casting couch" was first coined, in fact.

However, while Weinstein's rampantly misogynistic behavior is rightly an urgent topic of the moment, a clear example of the sort of unfortunately ubiquitous sexual harassment women both in and out of the Industry suffer every day, this "Weinstein Moment" permits an unusual opportunity to examine other behaviors attached to Hollywood's contemptible, but long-established behind-the-scenes "play for pay" transactions.

Let me be clear from the start: what follows does

not underplay, endorse or in any way minimize Weinstein's sexual crimes. It is an attempt to present my own opinions and observations concerning the Industry's real-life carnal transgressions, not all of which involve victimization. For instance, having sex with someone to advance your film or television or musical career is not always done unwillingly. On the contrary, numerous rising stars have been more than eager to seal a deal with something beyond a handshake. Yes, this is cynical careerism, and yes, it continues to exist—I can think of one major star who, despite his current screen persona as a magnetic ladies' man, actually jumpstarted his fame by willingly sleeping with a then-successful male director. The key word, of course, is "willingly." Which in this case does not equate to a major Hollywood producer begging a frightened starlet for a massage, and then threatening to derail her career if she doesn't submit. Still, a subculture of cold-hearted careerists willing to exchange physical pleasure for career advancement most certainly does exist in the entertainment business, and, one suspects, that helps embolden certain individuals to disdainfully brush off the protests of those who don't wish to play that game.

I do not make these statements lightly, nor do I make them without personal experience. From the early 1970's through the mid-2000's I was actively embedded in the Hollywood fabric, working as everything from a junior studio executive to a special effects supervisor, to a television producer. And I can tell you that during my career, I witnessed instances of power abuse—verbal, social, and physical. A dark hostility has always pulsed through Hollywood's underbelly, a sadistic undertone which rarely reaches the public's ears, but is wearyingly well-known to the unsung warriors who slog through Tinseltown's trenches. And sexual abuse is one of its manifestations.

As for Weinstein, his case has, I think, garnered such attention because it's involved so many brave and admirable A-list actresses who are now willing to speak out against their attacker's long-term aberrant behavior. Yet when it comes to dangling the promise of fame through fucking, Hollywood has always been an equal opportunity abuser. It's not only straight hetero men who proposition (or worse) straight hetero women: male on female harassment and abuse, female on male, male on male, female on female, and every possible gendered combination is fair game for Hollywood's ingrained practice of sexual coercion.

But, again, to flip from the unwanted to the willing: it's been my experience that regular, garden-variety prostitution factors in as well. Working girls and boys, some in the business, some not, are routinely devoured by certain stars and producers and executives as habitually and as often as other people eat breakfast. More than once have I seen a young woman or man whom I haven't recognized as belonging to the cast, or crew, or known entourage, disappear into a trailer during a lunch break, only to be replaced by another anonymous body a few days later. More distressingly, I've heard the horror stories of studio chiefs who essentially pimp out rising young actors and actresses to their friends and colleagues as part of some weird tribal bonding process.

Speaking personally, I still can recall an afternoon when, having completed taping for a Japanese television show I was then co-producing, a major Italian director stopped his limo in front of me. I was waiting for a hotel valet to find my own, much humbler vehicle. The limo's back door swung open and this director asked where I was going. He then offered to take me anywhere I wanted to go, assuring me that his people would take care of my car.

The invitation was clear. I declined. Not due to a panic attack at the homosexual approach, but because I understood what his offer really meant. I also understood the risks involved. This may seem either naïve or incredible, but despite the fact that I was in the film business for decades, I have been happily married to the same woman for over 40 years. So a major reason behind my turning down what probably would have been an interesting afternoon is the simple fact that I have never—ever - felt that any brief liaison was worth threatening the relationship I still so fortunately enjoy with my lifelong partner and best friend.

I've also, in my own small way, had to contend with unwanted female advances. During the mid-1980's I was once pursued by a major, slightly older female Hollywood power player, who subtly but consistently made a possible promotion contingent on "getting to know me better." That was an awkward one, indeed, because I had to work with this person on a near-daily basis, while gently but firmly signaling I was already spoken for.

I've found myself in the same discomfiting situation frequently, and I had to use the same tactic of gently but firmly saying no when hit on by men who were higher-up on the power ladder. In this way I can relate to women having to fend off unwanted male advances: such uncomfortable encounters usually left me feeling slightly soiled, confused, and embarrassed. Why, I would think, am I being put into this situation? What I am supposed to do here? How do I escape without harming my career?

My answer—and this only pertains to me—was to simply say no, and move on. I stayed consistent in my refusals, and, perhaps because I was raised in a law-enforcement family, always tried to second-guess and avoid any situation where I might find myself alone with a potential predator. That seems to have been the proper course, again, for me. However, I am a man, so a woman's escape tactics during such difficult moments is obviously a topic about which I cannot hope to fully know or address, not without seeming hopelessly arrogant or insensitive. I do know that I don't like bullying. Of any kind. To any gender.

Conversely, and to be completely candid, when it comes to extramarital Hollywood sex, I have been tempted. Once, while on location for a big-budget production, I was aggressively stalked by a lovely, smart, athletic young woman of my own age who definitely wanted a tumble. Or three. Thank God for (my ex-) Catholic guilt! By then I was, likewise, old enough to know that while illicit intimacy may be powerful enough to blow the back of your head off, such scenarios often end with someone sitting in a therapist's office. Or divorce court.

Interestingly, during that same location shoot, I watched a production assistant take up with a married above-the-line crew member. This starry-eyed young woman would regale me about the storybook romance she was looking forward to back in Los Angeles with her new, older lover. He promptly dumped her once production wrapped. During this same show, I also witnessed a major performer have her part slowly whittled down to nothing by a resentful director who was angry that she wouldn't sleep with him.

Luckily, all is not rot and corruption in the City of Angels: what I've previously described are the aberrations I experienced, not my everyday reality. The majority of Industry people I labored with during my career were sharp, serious, hard-working professionals with families and loyalties and principles of their own, just like the citizens outside the filmmaking world. Movie folk are also admirably grounded: they know there is no such thing as a free lunch, and it was to these tough, fine figures that I always gravitated. Today, I am honored to say that many of these same kind-hearted, admirably wised-up comrades remain my closest friends.

Still, I am afraid that the casting couch does, and will continue to exist. Why? Because demanding unwanted sexual favors is a smaller manifestation of our country's larger, ongoing, deeply troubling war against gender equality—a war which some men continue to wage by using fiscal threats and sexual coercion as anti-woman power tools.

Can things change? Will they? Let me conclude with the wise, insightful words of someone with far more cachet in this matter than myself, a woman who was harassed by Harvey Weinstein. That individual would be actor/screenwriter/producer Brit Marling *(Another Earth, The East,* the Netflix series *The OA).* In her distinctive *Atlantic Magazin*e essay entitled

"Harvey Weinstein and the Economics of Consent," Marling combined her own dreadful Weinstein-encounter with a penetrating, far-reaching examination of the sort of financial and cultural elements now existing in an America that continues to allow the Harvey Weinsteins of Hollywood to exist. As Marling so eloquently wrote:

"…The real danger inside the present moment…would be for us all to separate the alleged deeds of [Bill] Cosby, [Roger] Ailes, [Bill] O'Reilly, or Weinstein from a culture that continues to allow for dramatic imbalances of power. It's not *these bad men.* Or *that dirty industry.* It's this inhumane economic system of which we are all a part. As producers and as consumers. As storytellers and as listeners. As human beings. That's a very uncomfortable truth to sit inside. But perhaps discomfort is what's required…."

Paul M. Sammon is a noted film author who spent decades working in the film industry. He is best known as the author of *Future Noir: The Making of Blade Runner* (recently rereleased in a best-selling 2017 revised and expanded edition from HarperCollins). Additionally, Sammon has published film pieces in *The Los Angeles Times, Empire Magazine, The American Cinematographer, Cahiers du Cinema* and *Cinefex;* he is also the author of the books *The Making of Starship Troopers* (1997), *Ridley Scott: Close-Up* (1999), *Alien: The Illustrated Screenplay* (2000), *Aliens: The Illustrated Screenplay* (2001), and *Conan the Phenomenon* (2007).

Sammon entered the film industry as a publicist in the 70's, before becoming a producer, director, special

Lori Perkins

effects coordinator, computer graphics supervisor, second unit director, still photographer, electronic press kit producer, and Vice President of Marketing: Special Promotions for a major studio. Some of the films on which he worked include *Robocop, Platoon, Blue Velvet, Conan the Barbarian, Dune, Return of the Living Dead, The Silence of the Lambs,* and *Starship Troopers.*

In 1988, in Moscow, Sammon co-wrote *Stereotypes*, the first animated co-production between Russia and the United States. For five years he also was the American co-producer of a number of Japanese television shows, including the long running entertainment program *Hello! Movies* (1988-1993).

Sammon was closely involved with the 2007 Final Cut/25th anniversary rerelease of Ridley Scott's *Blade Runner* on DVD. Among his other contributions, he was extensively interviewed on camera for *Dangerous Days,* the definitive three and a half hour *Blade Runner* documentary. He also provided a DVD commentary for *Blade Runner's* legendary "Workprint."

Wall Street Assets

By Veronica Vera, D.H.S.
(Excerpt from her memoir in progress)

After graduating from college in 1968, I arrived in New York to get a job in publishing on the path to fulfilling my dream to be a writer. But as a woman, the first step to employment in any field of endeavor, especially publishing, was a typing test. In high school, I was in Section One: we were called "the intelligentsia", groomed to go to college. The kids who took the commercial course, less esteemed than I, were taught basic business essentials, such as accounting or how to type. My hunt and peck skills never flourished into real typing, and did not improve in college, despite editing the newspaper and the yearbook. Scores of 26 words per minute with 12 errors could not get me beyond the offices of any personnel director (today, Human Resources), so I wound up on Wall Street where I didn't need to type.

It has always been people's lives that interested me, their motivations, their psyches, and Wall Street was full of characters. The one I remember best was Sherman.

My first job was in 1969, at a small over-the-counter trading house. The office where I worked did not coincide with my expectations of what the world of high finance would be. I had imagined tomb-like offices filled with cigar smoke and men in pin-striped suits. Though a portrait of our dead founder greeted me each morning as I exited the elevator, and the anticipated 100 pound bronze bull rested on a mahogany table, that was where the similarity ended. My job was in "the back office," which was actually in front. "Back office" referred not to a location, but to the activities involved. On the front lines were the traders—the stars of the firm. Bringing up the rear were the people who worked behind the scenes, the (pre-computer) bookkeepers or, as Sherman called them, "the slobs."

"Crazy Sherman," a short, loud-mouthed Napoleon, was the head trader. His colleagues liked to say he should be trading in the head. I met Sherman my first official day on the job when I was summoned to the trading room. He interrupted his telephone conversations and a string of "fuck this" and "fucking that's" to check me out real thoroughly. He pricked up his ears and sniffed the air.

"What's your name?" He barked.

"Mary."

"Mary. A shiksa. Shiksa, do you like this material?"

He unzipped his fly, reached into the opening in his pants, and pulled out his shirt tail as if it were a penis. I fled the room. There were other women who told me that they would never even venture into his room, knowing his outlandish behavior. One told me "the firm lets him get away with anything, because he's the biggest money-maker." Crazy Sherman was the most disgusting person I had ever met—but to me, having come from my overprotected background, that made him exotic.

Sherman preferred to have female assistants do the job of writing up the trading tickets as he made the trades, and dial the phones quickly when he needed to buy or sell a lot of stock fast. The first day one of his three assistants was out sick, he invited me to take her place. I liked the action. It was a lot more fun than fighting with Sylvia, the near-blind bookkeeper, over whether or not the ruler I was using belonged to her. "You see, there's my name!" she'd whine, snatching away the ruler that she'd etched "Sylvia" on the back of, with her nail file.

Listening to Crazy Sherman trade, I learned more about the laws of supply and demand than I had ever learned at home or in school. I was a quick study, with a great memory for names and phone numbers. Sherman could tell I had a lot on the ball, and I could tell that he wanted to ball me. That was his word for it, "I want to ball you." Sherman wanted to ball everyone.

Shortly afterward, he invited me out for a date, and I accepted. Dinner, the theater, the works. This little hick, eager to shake off her hometown dust, was swept off her feet, literally, and right into bed at the City Squire Motor Inn in Times Square. The tongue that wagged all day when he was wheeling and dealing was just as energetic at night. In fact, sex with Crazy Sherman was a ball. He was a skilled cocksman, and a master at oral sex, something about which I was barely knowledgeable. I spent long delicious hours with my body attached to his cock or his tongue, and there was no typing involved.

It was on Wall Street that I learned sex was an economic commodity. Nowhere was this demonstrated more effectively than in Crazy Sherman's trading technique. He was a frustrated comedian who idolized

Don Rickles and had developed his own shtick. The majority of the firm's calls came from order clerks at the big board houses who sat in rooms of 60 to 100 tense men, young and old. Sherman based his success on the assumption that whether the callers were wealthy investment bankers or salaried clerks, they were all horny. His phone sex technique when something like this:

"Joe! Hello Joe, you old douche bag. Did ya' have your teeth fixed yet? - Man has more money than God and he smiles like Grandpa Munster. What can I do for ya', Joe? Y Systems? We're having a special on that this week. Y Systems is ten to a half... Half bid for 1000. How about paying me 5/8 for 1000, Joe? It's my birthday. Wait. Have I introduced you to the new girl yet? Mary, pick up the phone. She's a shiksa, Joe. Shiksa, pick up! What the...? She'll be with ya' in a minute, Joe, she's just putting on her panties. She's always taking off her panties, her bush is so fucking hot. Shiksa, say hello to Joe."

"Hell-O, Joe," I'd coo, embarrassed at first, but still playing along. After all, it was just a game....

"Hmm, you'd love to be over here sniffing her seat, ya' toothless bastid. C'mon, pay me five-eighths for the thousand. Sold to Merrill Lynch, 1000 Y Systems at ten and five-eighths and I thank you Joe, you're a gentleman. Shiksa, write up the ticket."

Yes, he was strange, and he was all mine... and his wife's. Well, we were the central women in his life. I eventually found out there were a lot of others—he was definitely doing my co-workers, too, though he swore he wasn't. I found out when one had to leave because she was pregnant.

Crazy Sherman was a lot to handle on a full time basis, but part-time, he was fabulous. We talked about him leaving his wife, and our living together, but we were both lying. At least, I know I was. Deep inside both of us were real happy with things just as they were. He gave me the City tied up in a red ribbon: an apartment on Sutton Place, a hefty salary plus expenses, my first trips to Europe and Las Vegas—though we never went there together, a white Camaro he dubbed "the cuntmobile," jewelry, the good life. Most of all, he appreciated my sexuality. Crazy Sherman was nine years my senior. Until meeting him, I'd had sex with only two boyfriends, both of whom were as repressed and inexperienced as I was. The first one dumped me immediately after I gave him my cherry. The next one felt gypped after we had sex for the first time and I admitted I wasn't a virgin. "Schmucks," said Sherman, offering me liberation in one word.

Crazy Sherman was my lover, protector and teacher at a time when I welcomed all three. The truth was I had come to town unprepared to live on my own. He was a gilded anchor as I set sail on the sea of ambition. From his mouth burst an explosion of chutzpah, a firecracker delivery of his unshakable belief in his own canons: his opinions and his abilities. That confidence was something I had yet to learn for myself, but that was something I would never learn from him. Instead, what I learned was dependence.

There were times when I considered it a mistake that my love life had become enveloped with my paycheck, and, at other times, I was glad of the combination. I had little time for reflection. Seduced by what I could buy, I avoided thinking about the cost to my independence, and to my self-esteem.

45

Sherman could be brutally honest, and when he wasn't being honest, I learned from that, too. The final blow was when he cheated on his mistress by making love to his wife. When their new baby arrived, I decided to depart. By the time I left, I was a sophisticated New Yorker.

What I wasn't, was a feminist. A part of my job was to go out for drinks with business prospects, sometimes in a group with Sherman, sometimes on my own. There was no sex involved, although some of these men lived in hope. My job was to make the fellow feel special just by spending time with him, no matter how boring he was.

There was an entire revolution taking place, and I didn't notice. If I had, I might have understood that my situation at work was sexual harassment, but the term had yet to be coined. It would be some time before the idea trickled down to Wall Street: a very macho place. When I was there, of the more than 1300 seats on the New York Stock Exchange only one was held by a woman, Muriel Siebert. She was considered an anomaly. While I was spending at Bloomingdale's, Betty Friedan, Shirley Chisolm and others were investing in themselves, forming a movement, and the structure of NOW.

There were other women too, women whom I would term mothers of sexual evolution: women such as Dell Williams, who, after a highly successful career in advertising, created Eve's Garden, the first women's sexuality boutique, and the indomitable artist and sex educator Betty Dodson, who would become one of my mentors. It was Betty, who in 1973 created a slide show for the women of NOW in which her drawings of women's genitals were held up for display. Five hundred women had assembled, and they burst into applause at the wondrous variety of what they saw. It was Betty, and Dell, and their sisters, who held space in the feminist movement for those of us who wanted to claim or reclaim the power of our sexuality, those of us who believed, or had always been told we were sluts. I needed that space in order to grow.

As I look back, I wonder if things have changed, and I fear they have not, but they should have, and I believe they can change from here on. So, your wise Godmom Mary Veronica offers these words of wisdom to young people today as you set out to find your way in the world.

1. Know that at the beginning of your career, you are viewed as fresh meat in the lion's den.
2. You will start at the bottom, but having the skills necessary will give you the means to work your way up.
3. Understand money. If you are dependent on someone else for the roof over your head, you can get boxed in.
4. Explore your sexuality, respect its power. Own it.
5. Respect your choices and own them. I don't regret my years on Wall Street. They were exciting and fun. I witnessed some historic New York moments from the front row. But I do wonder what I could have been doing elsewhere.
6. Don't be afraid to speak out, and don't be afraid to leave.

   And, to the Shermans of the world: The jig is up.

Lori Perkins

Veronica Vera is an artist, author and sex rights activist. After a few years on Wall Street she followed her dreams and began her writing career. For a dozen years she wrote hundreds of articles for adult publications, most notably, "Veronica Vera's New York," a monthly column about the sex life of the City published in *Adam Magazine*. She founded the world's first cross gender academy, *Miss Vera's Finishing School for Boys Who Want to Be Girls,* in 1989. She has authored three books about her academy, and the subject of gender expression. Her latest is Miss Vera's Cross Gender Fun for All (2016).

Veronica is a former porn star, and a member of Club 90, the first porn star support group whose members include Annie Sprinkle, Jane Hamilton (Veronica Hart), Candida Royalle (1950-2015), and Gloria Leonard (1940-2014.). She has testified for freedom of expression in Washington D.C. In 2014, she received a Doctorate in Human Sexuality from the Institute for the Advanced Study of Human Sexuality, San Francisco (IASHS), the first school to have offered advanced degrees in human sexuality. She is at work on an autobiography.

Contact: www.missvera.com
email: missvera@missvera.com.
Blog: veronicavera.wordpress.com.
Twitter: @MissVera212
FB: Veronica Vera; MissVeraDHS
Instagram: missveronicavera

#MeToo: A Rock'n'Roll Runaway
By Camilla Saly-Monzingo

I never want any girl to feel that she cannot defend herself against an unwanted attack. Teenage girls should not be coerced, forced or manipulated into having sex. They should feel strong enough inside themselves to choose when, how, where and with whom they want to have sex. They should possess the emotional agency to defend themselves, and they should always feel they have the right to say "No!"

In the 1970's, when I was a teenager, I was assaulted and coerced into sex many times. I was brought up to believe that women must always be polite, and that in order to be polite, one must acquiesce to men's desires.

Many teenage girls are unsure of themselves, and insecure in social situations. They want approval, want to be "cool" and be accepted by their peers, and may particularly want attention from older men whom they desire and/or admire. Teenage girls may be attracted to men who are older than they are: when I was 14, 15 and 16 I was much more attracted to men in their 20's and 30's than I was to boys my own age. In my case they happened to be men in rock'n'roll bands, but for many it could be a teacher, a family friend or an acquaintance, rather than a distant "idol."

This myth that men often cite, that the girls are hanging around, in my case in a club or backstage or in a hotel lobby, "because they want it," and that means "they were asking for it," has to be dissected, examined and addressed. I did want attention. I did want approval. I was a sexual being. But I did not want to be coerced, abused and raped. Those are very, very different things.

I was in sexual situations with men who were not brutal or coercive. Some of those situations I regret, some I do not, and I believe there was some joint responsibility there. The only caveat for me is that older men—and older people - have a responsibility to look out for younger people—especially to children and teenagers. Those men (or women, as the case may be) have the responsibility of seeing the teenager's "crush" as just that: an early blossoming of sexual interest which doesn't have to be reciprocated. They have the moral responsibility to recognize that teenagers in those situations do not have the wisdom and sexual agency to make wise decisions regarding their own sexual behavior. They are not emotionally equipped, and have not yet come into their full power as adults, thus their sexual judgment is impaired by their immaturity. Unfortunately for me, those I came into contact with were much more interested in reciprocating, especially when it came to a young girl who they thought was "hot." But I am not going to describe those incidents. I am going to describe the men who were predatory from the outset: those I was *not* attracted to, who forced their sexual advances on me.

I remember being physically carried into a bathroom and raped by a rock'n'roll roadie who was the friend (he called himself the "big brother") of one of my best girlfriends. We thought we were safe hanging out in his apartment. Apparently, "big brother" eventually got around to his "little sister" as well. She told me about that 35 years later.

I was raped by a guy who preyed upon me when I was a runaway, taking me to his apartment with the promise of money, and anally raping me—with no lube—'til I bled. For many years afterward I could still detect a small section of my asshole that had been un-puckered from that rape.

A guy working for a major drug dealer who supplied cocaine to Led Zeppelin and the Rolling Stones kept me and a friend trapped in his Bronx apartment for two weeks, drugging us with PCP and raping us every night while we were in a stupor. I finally got away from him because one day he took us to his friend's NYU dorm room, and I was able to sneak out while he was asleep, panhandling subway fare to get back home to my parents' house.

Yet another incident was with a guy who worked for the New York Dolls who coerced me into giving him a blowjob in a car, and then brought me back to his place for a very not-fun threesome. I was 16.

Oh yeah, and there was the time when I went up to this second-floor clothing store on 8th Street in the West Village. This fat, mafia-type guy was the boss there, and my friend "worked" for him—I'm not exactly sure how—and she set me up to take my clothes off for a photo shoot. He put me in high heels and some sort of garter-belt and stockings thing with a red feather boa and had me bend over. He insisted on making my asshole look wet—was it with his tongue, or with some lube? I can't remember—I just remember that awful feeling of wetness—I couldn't see what he was doing - and then he took pictures of me while he forced me to stand in this awkward, bent over pose. Yuck! I was must've been 14 or 15.

If I had felt more of a sense of self-possession in each of these situations, I may have been able to get out of them. It was my overall sense of helplessness and a lack of a feeling of my own power that made me unable to fight back. I simply didn't have those emotional and physical tools at my disposal.

Teenage girls need to be strong. They need to feel that sense of their own power physically, in their bodies. They need to have the emotional strength to get out of bad situations, to say "No!", to kick someone in the balls if they have to. We need to teach and nurture their development of inner strength, their sense of self, their power and their confidence. From that strength comes the ability to have your wits about you in dicey situations.

We also have to teach men that, when dealing with young people, what looks to them like "I'm into it" doesn't give them license to do whatever they want, regardless of the power and age differential. And it is never okay to coerce or force sex on anyone.

Only once did an older rock'n'roll guy, back then, look out for me. I will never forget it. I walked into Max's Kansas City—a rock'n'roll club in New York— wearing a short leather skirt, with a garter belt attached to stockings showing below the skirt line. This guy—I don't even know his name, I remember he had a mullet hairstyle—looked at me and said, "You can't wear that. Go home and change!" And you know what? I did. Thank you, anonymous rock'n'roll guy with the mullet. You were the one guy who did me right.

Later, when I became a teacher, I taught lots of kids, and some of them were Black and Latina "tough girls." They were the ones who began to teach me how to behave. I admired how they had a stance that indicated that they would "not take shit from no one." Around that time I remember being on a subway train, and there was a guy in a raincoat who was trying to rub up against this Black girl. She turned right around and said, loudly, "You touching me??" He backed right off. Wow, I realized. I could do that! Many years later I used the same technique when a man was following me from train car to train car. I said, loudly, "You following me??" He, too, backed off—and I guess found someone else to follow.

Somewhere along the line I developed a sense of my own righteous anger. That anger made me feel strong. It made me feel that I could fight off attackers, defend myself, that I could be as strong as they were. My sense of my own power enabled me to call out unwanted touching, to say "No," when I meant "No," and even prevent unwanted attention in the first place. Women would tell me they admired my confidence and ability to vocally call out behavior that I didn't like, and they also saw the being I had become: a sexually empowered woman who celebrates and honors her erotic self. They didn't know the long journey I had taken to get there.

Today I am fearless. Call me crazy, but I fear no man. I know we can all die in some terrible accident, or from some illness, or under unforeseen circumstances, but I feel strong in my body, confident in my mind, and emotionally equipped to deal with people who would try to belittle, intimidate, harass or otherwise sexually assault me. I'm 58, and I want to live in a world where all 15 year-olds feel the same way.

Camilla Saly-Monzingo is a lifelong New Yorker who grew up the Upper West Side in the gritty 1970's. A proto-punk, she was a "regular" at Max's, Club 82, and CBGB's, and worked for the Ramones, among other rock'n'roll bands. A high school teacher and teen mentor for 26 years, she now works as a writer and editor, and is actively involved in preserving New York City history and culture. She lives in Harlem with her husband, Mark, along with one bad cat and one good cat.

Consent: Breaking the Silence
By Mary Biliter

The summer before sixth grade, a distant family relative began staying at our house in Huntington Beach, California. I awoke one night to find him in my room with his hand on my breast. I panicked, but that didn't stop him. I told my parents, who blamed me because of a nightshirt I wore to bed.

I was 11.

Night after night I fought sleep, hoping if I stayed awake I could scream if he entered my room again. But he always preyed on me when I was asleep.

By my freshman year in high school I discovered alcohol, which allowed me to forget. I was new to public schools, having attended parochial schools my whole life. That year, I asked a sophomore football player to the Sadie Hawkins dance. He agreed, and I felt like the luckiest girl. Securing a date with a popular football player meant an inroad into acceptance and popularity. Or so I thought at 15.

Since he could drive, before the dance he took me to a pre-party. I didn't know what a pre-party was, only that the house was overflowing with teens and alcohol. We returned to the party after the dance, where my date led me to a back bedroom. We began kissing and I must have passed out because he called my name: "Mary, Mary."

When I opened my eyes, he laughed, but left. He didn't continue kissing me. What I took away from that first high school dance was that when I was too drunk to consent—even to a kiss, and he stopped.

By my senior year, my drinking had progressed, as had my alcohol consumption. I began drinking alone because I didn't like drawing attention to how much I drank. By the end of high school, I was a daily drinker. Before school started, I drank a fifth of Jack Daniels and loaded up on gum to mask my breath. At lunch, I popped 600 mg of NoDoz, an over-the-counter stimulant, which I washed down with 40 ounces of Olde English 800 malt liquor. After school and sports practice, I drank a bottle of Boone's Farm Tickle Pink. I maintained a weighted GPA of 4.3 because I was in Advanced Placement (AP) classes. My grades earned me "Senior of the Month," and my involvement in swimming and field hockey earned me letters.

The only days from school that I remember vividly are the rare days I didn't drink. Even though I drank alone, my behavior began to draw attention from one guy in my journalism class. I knew he'd tell my parents, so days I had journalism, I didn't drink. In the same class there was another guy who I hadn't noticed until we were partnered for a story assignment. He suggested we go to his house after school to write the story. I didn't think twice about his suggestion, and followed him to his house. No one was home. His notes were in his bedroom.

We sat on his bed to work because there was no

desk. When he leaned over and tried to kiss me, I was genuinely surprised. In that shock and nervousness, I giggled. Wrong move.

He was taller and stronger than me, and within seconds I was trapped beneath him, with my head pressed against the headboard. He held my wrists with one hand over my head and ripped my pink pants. My cries, shouts, and pleas to stop went unheard in the empty house. Pinned beneath him, I closed my eyes and waited for him to finish. When he did, I opened my eyes to find him smiling.

"I said, 'Stop.'"

"Did you?" he laughed.

A smug look crossed his face. "Oh, I'm sorry, I thought you wanted this."

As a drinker, I didn't have a great reputation for making good choices. Add to it, my active alcoholism eroded what little self-esteem I had. With ripped clothes, I ran out of his house, drove home and told no one. Who could I tell who wouldn't blame me?

The memory of that afternoon came flooding back when a friend called me in tears last week. She was at a get together with some new friends she'd met at college. She was asleep, when she was awoken because someone was touching her. Her utter shock and devastation that someone would sexually assault her while she slept were feelings I understood. After all those years, I grieved for what had happened to her and to me.

I told her about my freshman year dance experience.

"When one of the most popular guys in school stopped because I was too drunk to give consent, I thought all high school guys were like that," I said.

I then shared what had happened my senior year in high school.

"My biggest regret is that I never told anyone what happened to me," I said.

Telling this woman over the phone broke a 31-year silence.

I offered to meet her at the emergency room. I explained the role of a sexual assault nurse examiner (SANE), who is a registered nurse qualified to check for injuries that a person may not see, conduct a sexual exam and collect evidence from her and her clothes. I then spoke to her boyfriend, whose sole focus was on this woman's welfare.

She didn't want to "cause trouble." I reminded her that the decision to report to the police was entirely hers. However, by having a SANE nurse examine her, the sexual assault would be documented. If she chose to report later, she could. She ultimately made the choice to seek medical attention.

Living in Wyoming, a person who is unconscious is deemed to be "physically helpless" and not capable of consenting. In the simplest terms: if someone is asleep, regardless of the circumstances, that person cannot give consent.

According to results from a National Crime Victimization Survey, sexual assault remains the most underreported crime in the United States. I didn't tell anyone, let alone report it.

On today's college campuses, female students aged 18-25 are three times more likely than women in the general population to experience sexual violence.

This woman who called me and gave me consent to share her story is part of the most vulnerable population for these assaults. The National Intimate Partner and Sexual Violence Survey reports that nearly 80 percent of female rape victims are assaulted before the age of 25. I was 17. My friend is 18.

The United States Department of Justice reported that women are significantly more likely than men to be injured during an assault. One out of every six American women has been the victim of an attempted or completed rape in her lifetime. Nine out of every 10 victims of rape are female.

One of the most staggering surveys conducted by the Rape, Abuse & Incest National Network (RAINN) focused on what the sexual assault survivor was doing when the crime occurred. Forty-eight percent were sleeping, 29 percent were traveling to and from school or work, 12 percent were working, 7 percent were attending school and 5 percent were doing an unknown or other activity.

As the survivor of two sexual assaults, I can attest that they are physically debilitating, emotionally draining, unimaginably traumatic and shameful. There is no timetable for when someone will heal from a sexual assault. Tragically, it took a young woman's assault for me to begin healing from mine.

But it's far from over. If anything, by acknowledging my sexual assaults, I am more keenly aware of the systemic sexual abuse that happens to women.

If pubescent girls aren't protected in their homes, on the playground, or in school, how will they ever fend off sexual predators? The issue runs deep, but if girls and young women know what sexual abuse, harassment and assault look like, they will have a better idea how to combat it, and more importantly, report it.

My story began as an 11-year-old who was touched without consent and then left to deal with the aftermath. I know my story isn't unique. However, as more and more women raise their voices on systemic sexual abuse, it won't have to be another girl's story.

Mary Billiter is an award-winning weekly newspaper columnist, college writing instructor and romance author of the highly entertaining Resort Romance series. She also has novels published under the pen name, "Pumpkin Spice."

Mary resides in the Cowboy State with her unabashedly bald husband, her four amazing children, two fantastic step-kids, and their runaway dog. She does her best writing (in her head) on her daily runs in wild, romantic, beautiful Wyoming.

Read more about Mary and her work at: www.marybilliter.com. Follow Mary on Twitter: @MaryBilliter

Tit for Tat
By Katherine Ramsland

Situations of subtle compromise are probably the most frequent abuse of power, and the most difficult to identify as sexual misconduct, because the aggressor can easily say he was misunderstood. He slips away, leaving his target violated in a non-specific way. Even if she complains, it's difficult to make anything stick. She will also be labeled in some negative way, not to mention ostracized.

Here's an example from just a year ago: a good friend, A, introduced me to B, a business partner, because A believed B could open significant doors in my career. He left us to work it out. I've known A for many years. I trust that he acted in good faith and did not know what B was really like. B was a different story. He wanted to meet alone to go over the plan. He had a "good feeling" about our future association, which he said would keep me "very busy." He wanted to spend a day with me at my house. I resisted. He insisted. He was bringing things to show me and he needed a table to spread them out. A restaurant just wouldn't do, and he didn't want me to have to travel to his distant office. If I said no, it would be my loss. He'd find someone else. I gave in.

He arrived. He hadn't brought any materials. He commented on how nice I was to him. He'd "never felt so comfortable" with someone. He'd like to know me better. He moved close to kiss me. I backed away. I showed him a place to sit and I sat away from him, inviting him to tell me about the project.

He sat on the couch. He wanted me to sit next to him. I pressed again for details about the work, but he wanted to "get comfortable." I went over to the couch, but sat on the arm, keeping my knees as a buffer between us. He talked about how well we'd get along, if only I'd let him get "cozy" with me. "This is how things work in my world."

His words were vague, but his intent was clear. He reached for me, but I shook off his attempt to pull me close, and said, "Is this the price for a project?"

He got it. I wasn't playing. His face changed. He suddenly acted horrified by my interpretation. "I'd never expect that. I just thought we were getting along. What kind of monster do you think I am?"

He got up to leave. He assured me he would be in touch, to prove that he wanted to work with me. I never heard from him again.

There wasn't an assault. It wasn't even contact. Despite the obvious context of giving me entree into his business in exchange for sex, it was easy for this man to deny that there was any such overture. It was a slick move. But I felt sullied and disgusted. He saw neither my talent nor my experience. He saw only an opportunity to exploit my desire to work with him, hoping it would string me along long enough to agree to compromise. He thought I'd do whatever was asked. And it sounds like other females who worked with him did. But I didn't need the job that badly. I was fortunate to be rid of him. It could have been much worse.

But I still faced A, who wanted to know how it went. According to him, B was ready to offer me work and couldn't wait to get started. I knew better. I couldn't tell A what had happened, because it would have ruined his relationship with B (or with me, should he side with B). The incident had a negative ripple effect, making me trust A less. It's sort of like what Quentin Tarantino told the *Los Angeles Times* in the wake of the Harvey Weinstein scandal. He knew about some of the incidents of sexual assault and did nothing. "What I did was marginalize the incidents. I chalked it up to a '50s-'60s era image of a boss chasing a secretary around the desk. As if that's O.K. That's the egg on my face right now."

It's more than "egg." It's a complicit culture of males letting other males do whatever they want to women. It's females staying silent, and even enduring it for years in order to keep their status, opportunities, or employment. It's a culture in which Bill O'Reilly can settle a *sixth* lawsuit over alleged sexual misconduct for a historic amount, and still be given a lucrative contract to remain in his job.

The formula of sexual compromise is grounded in this culture of male sexual dominance. It goes like this:

Male: *I have something that you want. You have something I want. You can get it by giving me what I want. We will both be satisfied.*

The implicit idea, which males seem to accept, is that the woman wants it, too. However, the result is that the male remains in charge and gets what he wants, with no negative consequences. The female who gives in gets something, but knows that she acquired it through compromise, not merit. She has gained, but she also has lost. Sometimes, she has lost a lot. And the female who resists loses the opportunity.

So this is a slick maneuver. Aggressors can always pretend they were surprised by the target woman's misinterpretation. Either way, they win. They will either gain a sexual conquest, or they will walk away from this overture without a scratch.

What grows from within this culture is an attitude I described when I was writing *Inside the Minds of Sexual Predators*. It's called *narcissistic immunity*. It shows up in the most predatory people. You might see it in a CEO, a high-ranking politician, a celebrity athlete, and even an actor or artist, and you'll definitely find it in repeat offenders who take significant risks. They have a talent for rebounding from setbacks because they're certain of their invulnerability. This comes not just from their repeated success, but also from the knowledge that those who know what they're doing won't stop them.

The peculiar resilience of narcissistic immunity derives from arrogance and disdain. Narcissists possess a sense of superiority that allows them to exploit others for their own gain. Sometimes they believe their victims should feel "privileged" to have been selected. This attitude is a clinical disorder that distorts reality, because excessive narcissists are enveloped inside a cocoon of their own concerns that buffers them from what others feel.

Narcissistic immunity is a distorted notion about how the world works. They believe they're "protected" via their special status. They have a "destiny." They're "smarter" than anyone else, and even if they're caught, they're certain they'll slip out of having to pay for their acts: punishment is for ordinary people, not them. They think they can apologize and be given a second chance. (But make no mistake: they will *not* reform.)

The irony is that while they believe they're set apart from others, they desperately need others to affirm their superiority. They need conquests. They must hear from others about how great they are. They harbor grudges and blame others, and when they retaliate, it can be deadly.

Still, they can attract an entourage of admirers. They might have a terrific sense of humor or the ability to inspire others, or enough money to make others eager to be around them. Such relationships are a one-way street, with the narcissist reaping all the rewards.

So now that we're spelling out some of the types of sexual misconduct rampant in our culture, from Hollywood to DC, from the mailroom to the boardroom, from high school and college campuses to churches, where do we go from here? How can we shatter this complicity and inspire its protectors to realize that silence is not just "egg on my face"? It is as if they told the offender, "What you're doing is fine by me."

How do we turn it from "okay" to odious?

Oprah Winfrey has called the Weinstein scandal a watershed moment. As the various women came forward to tell their "me, too" stories, it triggered pain, anger, and guilt. Yet, she wants us to keep our eye on the bigger picture. This isn't just about one man using his position of power to make women yield. "If we make this just about Harvey Weinstein," Oprah said, "then we will have lost this moment."

Perhaps news commentator Gretchen Carlson, who accused Fox CEO Roger Ailes of harassment, will lead the way. She has worked with Democratic lawmakers to draft legislation that will make the process of filing sexual harassment complaints in the workplace easier and more transparent. Still, the bill will go to President Donald Trump, who is the target of similar allegations. It would be a landmark event for women, should this become law. It will take a movement of women who are "mad as hell, and aren't going to take it anymore," along with men who recognize the wrongfulness of males in power forcing such humiliating bargains.

We need to show respect for women who call out the men who do this, in the same way we have changed attitudes about such things as smoking, racism, polluting our environment, and accepting gender stereotypes. Let's hope we look back on this shake-up with relief, knowing that it helped move us forward, rather than feeling chagrined that things have stayed the same. Tit for tat, let's erode their power as they have long eroded ours.

Also, we must be more aware of predators' motivations. Successful predators prepare in advance. They consider all the angles of how they might get caught and how they can explain themselves, so it's difficult to catch them red-handed.

First, they set a goal. They know what they want and what it will take to get or achieve it. They have no mental inhibitions about causing damage or harm. They stay focused.

Second, they make a plan. The plan includes not just how to get what they want. It also includes escape routes: how can they get out if they need to?

Third, they compartmentalize well. They dispense with emotional attachments that might signal embarrassment or annoyance about being caught. They train themselves to give off no such signals so they can pivot easily into a different persona. Some suffer no remorse at all. By learning to pass themselves off as being just like everyone else—honest, trustworthy, emotionally engaged—they know how to act, both during their plan and during their escape. They recover in a split second, and slip their cover story into place with ease.

Their success depends, in part, on how well they study their targets. They have a different context for learning things. If they ask about your kids or dog, it's not because they're interested in you. They're interested in how to evaluate potential obstacles—or targets. They look for cues.

Because they study us, they know that most of us have a peculiar facility to block out things that we don't quite want to believe have occurred. (One actress described how a director told he needed her to remove her clothes so he could be sure she was right for a movie he had in mind for her. She wasn't sure whether to believe him or not.) We're vulnerable to falsehoods that are likely to match our perceptual frames.

Predators use deflection, social miscues, and misinformation to provide cover. Often, they use a contrived persona of charm and success to falsely engender trust. They remain relaxed, because their exit plan is in place. They expect it to work, so they don't get flustered. They give off few signals.

So change must occur on two levels: culturally and personally. Let's get educated on sexual predators, and on our own vulnerabilities, so that we can help the collective movement toward a better world.

Katherine Ramsland, Ph.D. teaches forensic psychology at DeSales University and has published 61 books, including *Inside the Minds of Sexual Predators.*

"I was only…"
By Catherine Gigante-Brown

He was my best friend's uncle. I knew him. I liked him. He was nice to me. He bought us
Italian ices from Vito's Pizzeria whenever he visited.

When Debbie's brother Michael spilled an entire waxed cup of Coke on my leg, I ran inside to get cleaned up. It was only Uncle Ernesto and me. I told him what had happened. He got a weird look in his eyes and said in an odd voice, "Let me feel how wet you are." Then he put his hand near my crotch.

It made me sick inside. I knew it was wrong. I knew grown men shouldn't touch young girls. "No," I told him and pulled away. He looked wounded, hurt. But I left anyway.

I was only 12.

"I was only trying to help," he called after me.

No. You weren't.

* * *

He ran the newsstand near the train station. I got off at that stop every day for my high school internship. He was nice to me. He told me how he'd lost his eyesight in a snowmobile accident when he was my age. I felt sorry for him.

Months later, when I told him I would be graduating soon, that I wouldn't be coming by anymore to buy my Tic Tacs, he seemed sad. He asked me if he could give me a good-luck kiss. I presented him with my cheek.

He roughly grabbed my face and shoved his tongue down my throat. I said nothing and pulled away. Then I walked down Lexington Avenue, angry tears streaming down my face. He was a nice blind man and I had trusted him.

"I was only trying to be friendly," he called after me.

No. You weren't.

It was a long time before I could trust a man again. I was only 17.

* * *

He was a stranger. I was on my lunch hour, rushing back to my part-time college job. I was wearing a loose cotton dress in pale lavender. I liked that dress—it made me feel pretty, confident.

I was crossing City Hall Park. Midday, it was crowded. Behind me, I heard one man ask another, "Where are we going?"

His friend answered, "We're following her. I like the way her ass jiggles when she walks."

That "she" was me.

Two men I didn't even know were talking about me like I was an "it," a thing. Like I had no feelings. I was minding my own business. I was only trying to get back to work.

I almost cried from embarrassment. But I forced myself to choke back the tears. I realized that I was more irate than ashamed. Instead of crying, I turned around and faced those men. And I saw red. For me. For all the other women who are objectified by a stranger and made to feel "less than."

"Stop talking about me like that," I told the man.

He sneered at me. "Freedom of speech," he said.

People were listening, watching. The park was crowded in the middle of the day. But nobody said anything to defend me. So I defended myself.

"It's not freedom of speech when it's my ass you're talking about," I told him.

I demanded that he apologize. His face flushed. His friend walked away, abandoning him. "I'm sorry," the man finally choked out. "I was only…"

But I didn't want to hear his excuses. I walked away, all the while, thinking, 'Was it me? Why did men think they could take from me? That they could talk about me, look at me, judge me, any way they wanted?'

I was only 19.

* * *

It is now almost 40 years later and things haven't changed very much. This sort of thing still happens. To me. To my nieces and goddaughter. To everyone. Why? Is it to make men like that feel powerful? Is it to bury their self-loathing?

I might never learn why men do these things. But I do know that it's about them, not me. They do it to famous actresses. They do it to semi-famous writers. And nurses. And trans people. The men who do things like this are in lofty positions like movie moguls, and they are in lowly positions like delivery boys.

I decided right then and there, as a teenager, that I

71

would always speak out, point out, write out, even shout out, if necessary. Just as long as I was heard. Because being heard was important. Being heard leads to people listening. Doing. It leads to change.

I believe "I was only…" are three of the most dangerous words in the English language.

"I was only joking."

"I was only trying to help."

"I was only…"

No. You weren't.

You only offer those weak excuses when you are caught.

Yes means yes. No means no. It feels good to stand up for myself. For my rights. For my body. At 19. At 29. At 58. And I am still doing it with words as well as deeds.

When will it stop? When we finally see each other as human beings. Period. Not by our sex. Not by our skin color. Not by our religion. Just as people. People with feelings. Rights. Boundaries. People who deserve better.

Respect. Kindness. Acceptance. It starts here. It starts now. It starts with us.

Brooklyn-born **Catherine Gigante-Brown** is a freelance writer of fiction, nonfiction and poetry. Her works have appeared in Ravishly, Huffpost Women, Time Out New York, Industry, Essence and Seventeen. She co-wrote the biographies Raw Talent and Whips & Kisses for Prometheus Books, and her short stories have been included in fiction anthologies, including the Herotica series. Catherine's novels, The El, Different Drummer and The Bells of Brooklyn are published by Volossal Publishing.

Me Too: Protecting Men from Themselves
By Kate Mara

"When my uncle tried to rape me (I got away) when I was 12, I told my mother (his sister), just like I was supposed to. She warned me not to tell my father, because he'd kill my uncle. She was right, he would have. But then I had to protect both myself and also my father, who would get himself in trouble if he knew.

"Then, since my uncle lived with my grandmother, every time after that, when I was sent to stay with her, I got to negotiate avoiding him without any adult support. She probably wondered why I shadowed her constantly, whenever I was there, during my teen years."

- Catherine M. Wilson

When I read this comment in one of the countless discussions sparked by #MeToo, something snapped. Or rather: Another piece of the puzzle fell into place. I had a visceral reaction to it, a sinking feeling in my gut. It wasn't the first comment along those lines. It is one of many. And I know what it feels like to be in that place, to have something terrible happen and not be able to turn to my family or friends because of what my experience would do to them. What it would make them do to others.

One of the many, many depressing patterns of the stories finally being told, finally being heard, at least by some, more than before, one of the many traps that help perpetuate the detrition of sexual assault is the need to protect those who would be supporting us. It's a different kind of "me too," one that hasn't got its own hashtag:

The need to protect (mostly) men from themselves. This isn't about those who assault us, about the predators, the ones getting away with it. I'm talking about the "good" ones, the ones who love us, who we love, the ones who frame their incapability of controlling their own actions as a desire to protect, and we understand that they mean well and we protect them instead of being able to trust them, to rely on them, to turn to them for support.

We protect them by shielding them from the knowledge of what it means to be a woman in this world; we protect them from knowing that this isn't something that happens to others, that it happens to us, and that we know who is doing it. We protect them because we don't want them to make things worse, we don't want them to settle us with the burden of knowing they did it "for us," because we don't want to live with the guilt of a "good" man getting into trouble for physically assaulting someone, not even a "bad" man.

We protect them because we can't trust them to be in control of themselves if we tell them. We can't trust them to center our needs over their own desire for violent retribution.

Don't be that guy who rapes, who sexually assaults women, who catcalls, who gropes, who makes sexist comments. But don't be that guy who cannot be trusted to deal with the reality of women being assaulted without resorting to physical violence, who cannot be supportive, not because he doesn't care, but because he needs to act out violent impulses.

The men who would go and beat up or kill the assaulter are participating in the cycle of silence and violence. They're keeping us from speaking our truth for fear of their inability to cope with our trauma. Don't be that guy.

As a woman on the streets since the 80s and on the Internet since the 90s, **Kate Mara** has seen her share of misogyny and sexism. As a media activist she has witnessed the power of speaking out and being heard countless times. Let's make this one of those times that lead to long term change. After studying film at the University of London she worked on documentaries such as *Into the Fire: The Hidden Victims of Austerity in Greece* and *Polyland*, about discrimination, defiance and dignity in Poland. Check them out!

Men, Women and #MeToo
By Jude M. Lucien

I'm reading lots and lots of experiences of harassment, assault and rape. These things are *always* wrong. They're equally wrong, no matter who is the victim or who is the perpetrator.

I'm reading a lot of things by men who have been sexually assaulted. Most of my man-friends have been raped. I care very much about that. I believe that men do not have nearly enough support for their sexual assault experiences. I believe that the patriarchy fucks both men and women, and that one of the primary ways in which it fucks men is that it makes sexual assault against men invisible. It makes it next to impossible for men to get support when they're sexually assaulted, or even to get any acknowledgement of their sexual assaults. And many, many men are sexually assaulted.

Likewise, women sexually assault people. They don't do it nearly as often as men do, and I attribute that to patriarchy (in other words, if women ruled the world, I think they might perpetrate many more sexual assaults, but they are subordinate in this world, so they don't do it nearly as much). But women *do* violate the sexual boundaries of both men and women pretty regularly. Women have violated my personal, sexual boundaries many times.

It is not at all my intention to minimize either the fact that men are sexually assaulted, or the fact that women sexually victimize both men and women. I just don't think that #MeToo, specifically, is about that. I think that #MeToo is about the pervasiveness of harassment, and the fear that constant sexual harassment engenders. I think that #MeToo is about the way that regular, daily sexual harassment literally structures our lives; it keeps women from riding in elevators with men, from walking alone in parking garages, or even walking on their own streets after dark. It structures the clothes that women wear, how much they drink when they're around men, and so, so much about how they date. I've never met a man who could even imagine the restrictions that most women take for granted. It also structures most of the warnings and safety tips with which we arm newbies in the kink community.

In the Pacific Northwest, in the winter, it gets dark at approximately 4:15 p.m. Growing up, I wasn't allowed to be outside after dark. My life outdoors was so limited by the threat of rape that I couldn't even play in the front yard after 4:15. Now, in contrast, the dark is where I'm the most safe.

In the dark, nobody can tell that I am what I am. In the dark, I look like a man, and I can walk my woman friends to their cars. They very often don't feel safe doing that. But we all know that I'm safest after dark. I asked my brother, this week, if he could drop me off at a particular bus stop on Halloween, after we trick or treat with his kids. He reminded me that this particular place is pretty sketchy; it's a crack neighborhood (where we grew up, and also where Macklemore grew up, if that's more meaningful). I told him that I do okay in those sorts of places, and he agreed, texting back, "that's because you're a bit dodgy." He's not wrong, that I'm a bit dodgy, but the primary reason that I'm not threatened by such places is that I pass for a man in the dark.

I got boobs at 11, and had them until I was 21. I over-exercised during my adolescence, and would take daily six-mile walks. Nearly every day I was catcalled, by adult men, from their cars. I escaped an attempted rape by my uncle when I was 12, so I was very aware that I'd been lucky to escape, and that those guys might, at any time, get out of those cars. That's what #MeToo is about. It's about the constant knowledge that the random catcall, comment or physical intimidation might turn into a rape attempt at any moment.

Women are trained to fear rape. We're sometimes trained by our mothers to try to avoid it, but regardless, we're *always* trained by early sexual harassment and assault, and by the fact that so many of our friends are raped, to understand that rape is a constant shadow looming over our lives.

Middle school was a gauntlet of bra snapping. You may think that's innocuous, but it's not. It's about boys regularly reminding girls that they're sexual objects. It's about boys regularly reminding girls that they can be sexually touched against their will at any time, and that everyone will laugh, and that nobody will intervene. I really didn't want to be a sexual object. I had big boobs. It sucked. Add that onto those adult men in cars, catcalling me almost daily, and reminding me that, like my uncle, they were bigger, stronger, and that if they wanted, they could rape me.

As a teenager, I also had a number of really positive relationships with boys/men. I certainly don't mean to imply that all boys/men participate in the harassment that structures the lives of women who are saying #MeToo. They don't. But every boy/man who witnesses the sexual harassment or violation of a girl or woman and does nothing *is* a participant.*

I came out at 15, but didn't actually start dating until I was 19, and since then I have had many women either violate my sexual boundaries, or try to violate them. My sexual interactions always include being on guard against sexual violation by women. I am in no way under the impression that women don't violate people sexually. They absolutely do.

Still, it's different. Women violate us interpersonally. Men also violate us interpersonally. But men's interpersonal violations are reinforced by those catcalls, those bra snaps, those attempted rapes, and a million other things that are a normal part of many, if not most, women's lives. Women's violations of both men and women are 100% unacceptable and inexcusable. They're not more okay; not at all, in any way. They are, however, different, because they don't have all that reinforcement outside of the interpersonal relationship. They don't have an entire social structure behind them that makes us fear them wherever we go. We don't have to negotiate our lives to avoid sexual violation by women.

I'm working toward a world in which men both

recognize and feel able to acknowledge, publicly, their sexual violation. I really want to support that. And I'm also really vocal about all of us who have been violated by women being able to recognize and acknowledge publicly that it has happened to us, and that women do that shit too. But I don't think that #MeToo is about that. I think that #MeToo is about the ways that the pervasive reinforcement of misogyny, through constant, daily sexual harassment,from adolescence on, structures women's lives.

At the end of the day, I believe that #MeToo is about how our lives are structured around fear. And I don't fear women. Neither do any of the men whom I know, even those who've been violated or raped by women. Fear of women just doesn't structure our lives, because when women violate us, it's a really fucked up *incident*. When men violate us, it's a tiny piece of the tapestry that's wrapped around us. In other words, it's just a tiny part of our fucked up, misogynist, normal lives.

That's the difference. Women have physically violated my sexual boundaries many more times than have men because my sexual relationships have always been with women. But all those years that men catcalled, bra-snapped, commented and attempted to rape me structured my life in a way that those women simply can't. So…well, I guess that's my #MeToo.

*I've definitely fucked up as a bystander. Most people do. It's entirely okay to fuck up. That doesn't make a person evil, at all. The right thing is to think about it and try to do better the next time that you're in that situation. I try to do that, when I fuck up. My wish for this #MeToo thing is that every man who has ever witnessed a sexually harassing moment will commit to himself to never again stand silently by when a woman is threatened, even if it is in the smallest way. That would be a real sexual revolution.

Jude M. Lucien writes about social justice, consent, identity, structural inequality and American culture. Her Ph.D. is in sociology, from the University of Massachusetts, Amherst, and she lives in the Pacific Northwest, where she grew up. She is butch, queer and white, and grew up working-class. Jude has been involved with various feminist, anti-racist, queer and socialist community organizations, since 1996. You may find more of her writing and contact information at http://judelucien.com

Every Book I Have Ever Written is a #MeToo Novel

By Trinity Blacio

I've been writing and publishing erotic romance for the past decade. My novels feature a woman and good, heroic, powerful, supernatural men against cataclysmic events that threaten their world, and the good men and my strong female characters always win. They are set in a "distant" world of vampires, werewolves, shape-shifters, aliens, and gods.

People always ask how a woman from Ohio can come up with these out-of-this-world situations. They ask me, "Where do you get your ideas?" This #MeToo moment made me realize that all of my heroines are, in fact, me, standing up to my predators. Every novel I have ever written is a #MeToo novel, and I've written over a hundred novels.

As writers, our experiences lay the framework for our stories—well at least mine do. That's why they tell writers to "write what you know." Unfortunately, I know abuse and harassment well. In my fiction, I have taken my life experiences and retold them as story. The female characters in my fiction are all survivors, each growing stronger from her own trauma, each refusing to be a victim again.

It's no surprise that I've had more than my share of sexual harassment and abuse.

The first time I can remember would be from my stepfather when I was eight. He showed me sex toys when my mother was at work. He would lay in bed naked wanting a massage. I remember the bathroom door lock was gone, and him walking in when I was taking a bath. Is there more? I don't know. I can't remember, but this is what sticks out in my memory. I really believe this one situation of always being watched and inappropriately desired formed who and what I write about. I could have withdrawn from people, but instead I got stronger to deal with it. My characters always show their strength in the end.

The second time was a on a date set up by my own father. At age 15 I was living in a new state with my father. My date and I were supposed to go to a movie and then back home. I can't remember the name of the movie, but I can remember the long drive down a road in the bluffs of Minnesota to a run-down cabin, and me screaming "No!"

Oh, he delivered me home, but that wasn't the end of it. I thought for sure I had gotten pregnant. My father found out, and let's say it wasn't pleasant on my end, until he found out what had really gone on. I never found out what happened to the said 20-year-old, but I do know he lost his job. He wasn't there at my father's car dealership the next time I visited him.

The situation still pisses me off each time I think of it, even now. First off, because my own father initially didn't believe what had happened to me, and second, because it was just brushed under the table. Nothing was ever said. Oh, the man lost his job, but there were no consequences. I was patted on the head, and nothing more was done. Even when I asked what happened to said man, I was told it was taken care of, and not to worry about it. Hence, in my novels, I make sure my bad characters get what they deserve.

No one suggested I report anything. No therapy was offered, and no support group. Mom was in another state with my sister, so I couldn't talk to them, but I was lucky my stepmother was there when no one else was. To this day my stepmother and I have a special bond, even though she isn't married to my father anymore.

I have written my novels to create a world where women support each other, not fully understanding what I was doing. My novels are fantasy, but this #MeToo groundswell has shown me that we can create a real world in which we have each other's back, and the next little girl whose stepfather makes inappropriate advances can tell her mother. Or she can tell her father she was date raped, and know that she will be heard, and that there's a system in place to stop the abuse from happening again.

And if for some reason she doesn't have those options, perhaps she'll read a novel where she'll see her reflection and know that she will survive, and, maybe, save the world.

Trinity Blacio is the #1 Amazon bestselling romance writer of paranormal erotic romance for the series *Running in Fear* and *Masters of the Cats*, as well as a number of dark fantasy, erotic romance, erotic horror and ménage titles. She is a PAN member of the Ohio chapter of Romance Writers of America, and is the bestselling author of a paranormal stepbrother romance series that made her an All Romance eBooks and Siren bestselling author.

Coming from a split family, Trinity Blacio has lived in Minnesota, California, Michigan and Florida, but eventually settled in the state where she was born—Ohio. She has an associate's degree in psychology and social work from Lorain County Community College, and a bachelor's degree in psychology from Cleveland State University.

You will find her on Facebook, Twitter and Goodreads. She loves to talk with all her fans.

#NotMe's Instead of #MeToo's
By Nikki Prince

I was molested by a family member and by a family "friend," all before the age of 10. It didn't feel right to me. However, I didn't have a voice to say "Stop." There is nothing worse than being voiceless and unable to cry for help because you're told this is what is supposed to happen to you. You are supposed to feel helpless. You are told that what he is doing to you is supposed to feel good and you'll like it. You're supposed to hold in your screams and let someone violate your very being, because, after all, it was a family member and a family friend. It wounds even deeper because the violation was done by someone that should have been trustworthy.

I kept silent about it until I was in my late 20s. The fear of not being believed is real. This is why we don't say it happened to us, because we know there are those who think we are making it up. We aren't, it happens more than it should, and more than you think. Talking about it helped some, but there are still times I have dreams where there is something in my mouth and I can't scream or talk. There is no way to get help. To take what isn't yours, to touch a body and to violate it whether it is just once or a million times, is a rape of a soul.

My soul was damaged the moment it happened. Who I am was damaged, but I've risen above that. I think that there has to be a way to put a stop to this. What happened made me who I am today, but that wasn't the perpetrator's right to change me. Whether it is touching someone inappropriately, or whether it is suggestive talk that isn't asked for, and, most definitely, if it is rape, it must stop. I hate that we have to have a #MeToo. I wish we didn't, but, the fact of the matter is, we do.

I have a daughter and a son whom I love and adore. I never want them to feel as I've felt growing up and having my body used against me. I never want them to feel the pain or the shame that comes with it. What can I do? I teach both of my children that their body is their own, and to know their rights. I tell them that they have a voice and to use it. I teach my daughter that she is beautiful as she is. That her body is her own temple and she has the right to choose what to do with that temple. She also knows that she should respect others' bodies. As for my son, I'm also teaching him that his body is his own and that he should never take what isn't his.

We must start with our children. Let's educate them to know their rights as human beings. Let's teach our daughters and sons that they don't lack agency. They need to know the difference between consent and non-consent. They also first need to love themselves. If a child loves themselves and knows their own worth, they'll know what they wouldn't like done to them. If they know that, they will know not to do it to others.

They need to know their body is their own, and to respect and know that the same goes for others. This needs to be taught at home and reinforced at school. They spend more time at school than they do at home.

I will teach my children to love themselves enough that they know what feels good and what doesn't. They don't have to live with the shame that a lot of us have lived with if we teach them from an early age what to accept and what not to accept.

This is the promise I've made to myself, to my children, and to the world:

Never again will I remain voiceless.

This is for me, this is for my children, and this is for the world to hear. We are here, we are the #MeToo's, and we will not remain silent ever again. Let's make a world where there are #NotMe's instead of #MeToo's.

Nikki Prince is a single mother of two whose passions lie in raising her children as readers, as well as gaming, cooking, reading and writing. While she has worked in law enforcement for most of her adult life, she also has a MA in Creative Writing with a concentration in fiction, and is working on a second MA in English. She is the president of the Passionate Ink chapter of Romance Writers of America (RWA). Nikki is a multi-published author whose work has appeared in several e-publishing houses. She loves to write interracial romances in all genres, but wants to let everyone know to not box her in, because there is always room for growth.

Not Them Too
By Louisa Bacio

"Are those $1,000-a-night fuck-me pumps?" It was my first job out of grad school at a real magazine publishing house, and he was the vice president of advertising. We were together in an elevator. What do you say?

At that time, nothing. Worse yet, I probably giggled or did something equally embarrassing.

Sadly, it wasn't the first time, and it wouldn't be the last time I'd experience sexual harassment or discrimination based on my gender.

With 30 magazines and more than 200 employees—98% male—the editorial director told me I wasn't allowed to travel for work simply because I was attractive and female. They didn't want to open themselves up to sexual harassment complaints. What about sex discrimination?

In the more than 25 years the company had been around, they'd never had a female editor. It wasn't until that point that I realized what "glass ceiling" meant. At the end of my five years with the company I was managing director of five magazines, and I was told that no one had ever written for as many of their magazines as I had.

It's not only men who perpetuate some of these issues, unfortunately. At another magazine an older senior editor called me into her office on my first day. She explained that, in publishing, there's only "room" for one female editor, and it was going to be her. That troubled magazine went bankrupt, and when the doors closed there was only one female editor: It was *me*.

During college I worked, one holiday season, at Victoria's Secret. Dress code dictated skirts and pantyhose—thank goodness I don't have to wear those anymore—and high heels. When I got the job I asked if there was a skirt length requirement. Nope, anything goes. Then I was sent home for my skirt being too short. Really?

As one can imagine, the customers could be pretty "edgy"—to put it in nice terms. One father and son came in asking for help finding a gift. "If she doesn't work fast enough, we can always whip her," the father joked. They both laughed.

I've been followed to my car—more than once—late at night. Fortunately, I've learned to be well aware of my surroundings, and I jumped in quickly and locked the doors. "I won't hurt you," the guy said, pulling on my door handle. "I have money. I just want to talk to you." I got out of there as fast as possible and called the police. Because next time, the woman may not have gotten away as fast.

Only once did I attempt to walk to work. It was a short hike down the Pacific Coast Highway in Laguna Beach. In a span of 20 minutes four cars pulled in front of me, blocking my path, offering rides. The drivers were all male.

But maybe they were just being nice.

On dates, a few guys got a bit too friendly. One "octopus"—as I still remember him—held the back of my head so tightly I couldn't move, in order to kiss me. Yeah, that's sexy, and no thanks, I won't be going out with you again.

Perhaps the scariest occurrence happened in my own home.

"Can we look at your roommate? Is she pretty?" A man's voice woke me in the middle of the night. I was 23, in grad school. "She's asleep," my roommate said.

"It's all right. We won't do anything. Just look at her."

I lay in bed, listening to footsteps come down the hallway, and stop outside my closed bedroom door. The doorknob rattled, and turned.

At that moment, I jumped out of bed, yanked on the handle, and screamed: "What the **fuck** do you think you're doing? Get out of my house!" I chased them out, and evicted my roommate the next day. She had flirted with two guys in a car, let them follow her home, and invited them in.

So yes, #MeToo. Too many stories, and I know many others have experienced much worse.

As a mother of girls, now, I've already noticed how some men react around my ten-year-old daughter who is a dancer. Yes, she's already as tall as me, and shapely. During competitions and performances she wears make-up, and looks older. But not that much older! Ultimately, she wants to go into the entertainment industry.

Opening the dialogue of #MeToo empowers women. I didn't let any of those incidents define me or stop me from doing what I wanted. I pushed through the adversity, and now I'm teaching my kids how to stand up for themselves. Hell no, not them too!

Maybe in the future, it'll be true.

Louisa Bacio, a Southern California native, can't imagine living far away from the ocean. The multi-published author of erotic romance enjoys writing within all realms—from short stories to full-length novels.

Louisa shares her household with a supportive husband, two daughters growing "too fast," and a multitude of pet craziness: Two dogs, five fish tanks, an aviary, hamsters, rabbits, guinea pigs and hermit crabs. In her other life, she teaches college classes in English, journalism and popular culture.

Contact Details:
Website http://www.louisabacio.com
Facebook: http://www.facebook.com/louisabacio
https://www.facebook.com/Louisabacioauthor/
Twitter: http://www.twitter.com/louisabacio

Why We #MeToo
By Jennifer Wedmore

When I saw the first #MeToo post on Facebook I thought to myself, "I am not posting that. I don't qualify, what happened to me wasn't the same thing." Then I realized that is exactly why I needed to speak my piece.

I was sexually molested for ten years. I became two people, the one who suffered during the night/early morning, and the one who got up and went to school and functioned normally. In high school a guy thought it funny to just reach around and grab my breast as I opened my locker. I ignored it: the catcalls from early age to adulthood, the casual brush against my backside as men moved by me, the reaching for something and "accidentally" brushing against my breast, the neighbor kid who thought it was okay to kiss and touch me whenever he wanted.

Our society kept this hush hush. We didn't speak of it. It wasn't happening, and it wasn't a big deal if it was addressed. Even if convicted you could just pay to get it off your record and it was no big deal. Life goes on, right?

The everyday fear women have of walking to our

car by ourselves or walking by a group of men must stop! We should feel safe in our environments! I have two daughters, and I dread them growing up, knowing they will go through all of this and accept it, as we all have. I am afraid to ask my teenager if she has experienced it. I fear nothing will ever change.

Women must stand together. Be strong. We must speak out!

#IBelieveYou
#WeAreOne
#PrayForOurDaughters

Jennifer Wedmore requested that the publisher not share her biographical details.

Until When? #MeToo
By Gen Ryan

#MeToo. These words over the past few weeks have taken on a greater meaning. It was once a simple reply; now it's so much more. I watched as my Facebook, Twitter and Instagram newsfeed filled with posts titled #MeToo, and stories of sexual harassment that left me speechless.

So many strong and powerful women came forward about their own experience with sexual harassment. I admired their courage to speak out, but more so I was sad. This is the world that I am raising my ten year-old daughter in: a world where over half of my Facebook friends have had at least one experience, if not more, with sexual harassment. As a psychologist and an educator, I can't help but stop and think of ways to end this. I don't want my daughter to be a #MeToo: to worry what she did wrong to warrant attention when it wasn't asked for. In the face of a world where #MeToo is more prevalent than not, something must change.

The problem isn't with women not coming forward, because as we have seen recently in the media that women are flocking and coming together more than ever. It's how, as a society, we view the female. How society takes our words, clothes, past sexual histories and scrutinizes them. This isn't about how many people a woman has slept with. Or how short her skirt was on the day her boss decided to touch her without consent. It's about our given rights as people who are female to demand respect both physically and emotionally. We should be able to dress for a night out with friends, and not worry that because we wore a little extra mascara someone will get the wrong idea.

We are not what we wear, who we date, or the one bad choice we may have made in high school or college. We are strong, powerful and beautiful. So if, as a society, we stop villainizing the victims, and start holding the individuals accountable for their actions, #MeToo will become a thing of the past. I hope that all women will continue to share their stories, band together and show the world that we are fierce and formidable and will not be silenced.

Until then, #MeToo.

Gen Ryan is an international best-selling author who spends her days as a forensic psychologist filling the minds of college students with everything they need to know to be good at their jobs, from profiling to interrogation, and ending with her absolute favorite, serial killers. Her nights, however, are spent crafting stories that will tear a reader's heart out and twist their minds at the same time. Follow Gen Ryan on Instagram at authorgenryan.

Doing What We've Always Done:
Gender Roles and Sexual Assault
By Carmela Caruso

I was pressed defensively into the corner of my couch while a man who hours earlier I would have referred to as a friend was straddling me, trying to pull my legs apart, and saying, "Come on. You know you want me to eat your pussy."

I was a modest, quiet, introverted 31-year-old who lived alone in a small town where many people moved to enjoy their retirement. I was not supposed to be sexually assaulted in my own home by someone I passed regularly while walking to work.

That is what I thought later when I tried to piece together how it had happened. Growing up in a city just outside of Boston, I had always been cautious. I looked over my shoulder, carried mace in my purse, and planned to fight for my life if I needed to. I thought rape and assault happened to women in dark alleys by perpetrators they had never seen before.

I learned later that 84 percent of sexual assaults are committed by someone known to the victim—friend, family member, acquaintance, or co-worker.

I knew him like most of the people who

frequented Main Street in the small town where I live. We were on a first name basis, would wave and say hello in passing, and could list a handful of details about each other recalled from our brief conversations.

He invited me to join his friends around the table of an outdoor café one night as I was walking home after work. He was originally from Chicago, and talked with an urgency which shifted from one subject to another with a dexterity I hadn't heard in years, since moving to the South. Both familiar and dangerous, I felt simultaneously lost and at home as I struggled to keep up with the conversation.

His friends left, and we relocated to a bar when the café closed. I drank water while he nursed a few beers. We spent hours talking together before leaving to join the event happening a few blocks away. When we arrived the band was finishing their final song, and the vendors had already begun closing down. He offered to walk me home.

I'd enjoyed the night talking to him, I was attracted to him, I wanted to see him again, but I was not ready for or open to the kind of contact walking me home would imply. I declined.

He persisted. I spoke directly. "I don't want you to walk me home. I don't want to have sex with you." He slung his arm across my shoulders, assured me sex wasn't his intention, and followed beside me as I walked toward my house.

Tracing back my steps that night, I see how I allowed myself to become trapped. I could have stayed downtown, refused to let him walk me home, stood more strongly beside my own no. My boundaries were like chalk lines drawn in the rain. "Don't cross this," I say, as it washes away in my own defenselessness. If I'd seen another woman in the same situation and she'd given me even a glimmer of indication that she was in trouble I'd have stepped in, voice raised, poised to call the cops or send fists flying if necessary. For myself, I unlock my front door and watch as he follows me in.

He went immediately to my spare bedroom and crouched down by a bookcase. When I moved in and stood behind him he rose abruptly, and pushed me backwards into the wall. He began mashing his face into my own, smothering me with sloppy, teeth-baring kisses.

He stopped long enough for me to choke out, "I don't want this," as he grabbed my wrists and began dragging me toward the bed. I bent my knees and gripped the ground with my bare feet. "Stop resisting," he said pulling me across the floor.

He let my wrists drop, then slithered seductively across the bed. "Come here," he said, his voice suddenly soft.

Had he been a stranger, an intruder, I wouldn't have hesitated to grab my cell phone and run from the house to call the cops. The familiarity, the friendliness of the past few hours created a buffer that prevented me from seeing the seriousness of the situation, which made me trust he wouldn't try anything else. Instead of leaving, instead of fighting, I walked into the other room and sat with my legs crossed beneath me on the corner cushion of my couch.

He came and sat beside me at first. He made it clear he was looking for casual sex. I told him I was looking for a committed relationship and was not interested in sex without one. We went back and forth for a while, getting nowhere, repeating our differences. I thought he would give up and leave. Instead he slung one leg over mine, pulled up my dress, and began trying to wrench my legs apart. When he moved to kiss me, I stacked my arms in front of my chest and held him off.

In the moment I saw him grasping my legs, saw the flesh of my thighs exposed, but I couldn't feel anything. Not the pressure of his hands on my body, not fear, not anger, just a dream-like numbness. I remember looking down at the edge of black fabric against my pale skin and thinking, "This is how rape begins."

He struggled, but couldn't pull my legs apart. He sat beside me again, defeated, then rose to leave. I walked to the door, pulled it open, and gripped the handle as he grabbed my ass and pressed his lips into mine before crossing the threshold. "If you change your mind," he said, "you can find me on Facebook."

After he disappeared into the darkness I double locked the door and went to the bathroom to scrub soap across my face. I shut off the lights and curled up into a ball on my bed. I could still taste his tobacco on my lips. I wondered if I should call the cops. I lay awake listening to noises in the night, afraid he'd return.

He didn't come back and I didn't file a police report, but I continued to see him regularly along Main Street in the small town we shared. He acted as if nothing had happened. When I passed him on the street he called to me with a self-assured confidence. I oscillated between freezing completely and responding automatically with an empty greeting.

Two months after the attack I passed him by and he moved to follow. He caught up to me easily and matched my pace.

"You never found me on Facebook," he said.

"Why would I?" I asked. "I felt like you sexually assaulted me."

He stopped short, took a long drag of his cigarette, locked eyes with me and said, "Really?"

As I stammered to repeat myself with more assurance, I could see that he was genuinely surprised. He took another drag of his cigarette and apologized.

He said he'd been in a similar situation many times before and found women thought they should act distant and unavailable to avoid being labeled a "whore" or "slut" for wanting sex. Men, he said, were expected to show force to which the woman, throwing down her feigned resistance, would respond. It's what women wanted, he said.

You don't have to go far to find evidence of this dynamic playing out in popular culture. In movies, TV shows, and books women are distantly seductive, men forceful and forthright. It's a structure of relating long-ago woven into our culture, and it's long-since been time to erase it.

I understand now why 84 percent of women who are sexually assaulted know their attackers. The lines between friends, acquaintances, and co-workers are blurred by society's expectations of us. Men, especially those in positions of power or influence, exert their "manliness" with the kind of sexual advancements that are prevalent in popular culture.

Women remain silent because we know the statistics, we know that most cases won't make it to court, and those that do won't win. We remain silent because we know our actions will be dissected until the assault becomes our fault, not his. We remain silent because in a society where gender inequality still exists, we know speaking out could cost us the advancement we've worked hard to get, the reputation we've built, the credibility we carry.

This is not to say that all men are remorseless predators, or that men are not ever sexually assaulted by women, but it is to draw attention to the behaviors society has made okay. Although it may be expected that men catcall, touch inappropriately, and have forceful sex with women, it is not and never has been okay.

We as a society have a long way to go to eliminate the gender roles that many of us have easily slipped into. Drawing attention to unhealthy dynamics and speaking out are the first steps to enacting the kind of shift that needs to happen for us to be safely and honestly ourselves, in relationship to each other. We must stop silencing the voice within us that knows when things are not okay. We must stop listening to the messages that movies, TV shows, magazines, and song lyrics send about gender dynamics. We must not be afraid to speak up, to speak out, to set boundaries and have them be honored. The responsibility for change rests not just on men, but also with women. It's time for all of us to put an end to the violence that we've perpetuated against ourselves and others.

Carmela Caruso believes in the power of words to enact social change. She lives simply, loves fully, and strives to have a positive impact on the world. Her work has been published in *The Watermark*, *The Cimarron Review* and *Elephant Journal*.

For Men the 'MeToo' Movement Should Be More Than a Hashtag

By Ivan Natividad

The Internet, amazing as it is, can sometimes seem like a revolving door for social issues and charities competing for our philanthropic affection.

On social media particularly there is a Kickstarter or Go Fund me campaign for anything and everything you would like to dole out the dough for, from backing the latest tech product to building schools in a third world country.

And then there is the hashtag… Formally known as the pound sign.

With hashtags, social media spammers can key in on terms to promote anything they want. Like last week when product spammers would use #LoboFire or #McCourtneyFire to get their products seen by people trying to search for posts about the actual fires. So lame. They are the Internet equivalent of looters who scoured homes in fire evacuation areas… Vultures.

Needless to say, popular hashtags often come and go with the changing tide of the online zeitgeist, and can often seem annoying. But the hashtag has also become a powerful vehicle to bring light to significant social issues and causes.

The latest "#MeToo" movement in particular has brought more awareness and support to female victims of sexual harassment and assault.

The "Me Too" movement started more than 10 years ago when Brooklyn-based youth activist Tarana Burke used those two words as a rallying cry to support young women who had survived sexual abuse, assault and exploitation.

A way to let them know that they were not alone.

In the wake of sexual assault allegations against veteran movie producer Harvey Weinstein, #MeToo gained prominence on social media recently when actress Alyssa Milano tweeted a call-out to victims "so we might give people a sense of the magnitude of the problem."

According to the Rape, Abuse, and Incest National Network, every 98 seconds someone in our country is sexually assaulted, and one out of every six women has been the victim of an attempted or completed rape in her lifetime.

Moreover, 90 percent of adult rape victims are female, and females ages 16 to 19 are four times more likely than the general population to be victims of rape, attempted rape, or sexual assault.

Within 24 hours of the #MeToo movement, more than 12 million Facebook posts, comments and reactions were made.

I have personally seen various posts from female friends who I have known for many years, coming forward and sharing specific instances of sexual violence they have experienced in their lives.

Others simply posted the hashtag without sharing, which is completely understandable.

These women are showing courage to let people know that yes, they have been the victim of some form of sexual violence. It's amazing.

As a man, the movement has made me reflect on my own experiences. When I was a single young man I had a somewhat healthy nightlife, often frequenting clubs and bars wherever I lived. And yes, I have been groped or touched in a sexual way without my permission. But to be honest, personally, it didn't bother me. In those instances I either shrugged it off, or, as a single adult, took them as inviting advances that eventually became mutual.

But unlike many women, that's because I had the privilege of never really feeling like I was in danger. Never did I worry about being followed down a dark alley afterward. Never did I worry about a woman stalking me at my home or place of work because I did not reciprocate their advances.

The possibility of being sexually assaulted or raped is not something that ever enters my brain. Based on the statistics, these are privileges I know I have as a male. And that is why it's been very disturbing seeing how some men are reacting to the #MeToo campaign.

"No one I know has ever done that to a woman. The statistics have to be exaggerated!" Yes, and the world also revolves around you as well. Good for you.

"Well I have daughters and a wife now, so I can't stand when I hear about women being sexually assaulted." So it took you to have daughters to realize that something was wrong here? … Good for you.

And then there is #NotMe, a hashtag in reaction to #MeToo that some men are using to let the world know that "No, not me! I've never sexually assaulted anyone!"

So you're celebrating the fact that you're not raping women? Way to raise those expectations! Good for you.

And then there is the guy who is going to go around liking all of his friends' #MeToo posts, not reading them and calling it a day. Come on fellas. We can do better than that.

Women are proclaiming "MeToo" and coming forward to tell the stories of their abuse to highlight the magnitude of the issue, while finding a sense of support from other victims and their allies.

This campaign isn't about the men who don't commit sexual violence; it's about the ones that do, and the culture that we condone as men that allows them to get away with it, as only six out of every 1,000 rapists end up in prison.

As men, we cannot stay silent on an issue that affects the daily lives of nearly half of our population. Does that mean we have to go and seek out rapists and cat-callers?

No, but we can stop supporting or condoning a culture that hyper-sexualizes women.

We can stop shrugging off actions and conversations that commodify women in a way that perpetuates sexual violence.

When we see another man randomly grab a woman's ass in a club, we can say something.

We can redefine our own masculinity to detach it from abusive stereotypical behavior.

Our character is based on what we do, not what we think we believe.

For fathers, setting that positive example for our sons can go a long way toward letting them know that behavior which demeans or violates women is unacceptable.

And maybe by the time they are our age, #MeToo will have been more than just a hashtag.

Ivan Natividad is the Digital Editor at *The Union Newspaper* in Northern California, where this article appeared on October 20, 2017.

For Guys Reading #MeToo Testimonies

By Courtney E. Martin

First, read the #MeToo stories on your Facebook or Twitter feed.

Read about the bosses and teachers and neighbors and friends who have sexually harassed and assaulted the people you know and maybe even love. Pay special attention to the stories. You will see patterns. You will shudder at the abuses of power. You might even feel sick to your stomach. Then immediately…

Do nothing.

Sit in silence. Don't say anything. Don't retweet anything. Don't text anyone. Just sit there. Maybe even close your eyes. Feel what you feel.

I'm guessing underneath the surprise and the anger (anger is easy), there is a deep well of sadness that you live in a world where women are treated this way. Like objects. Subhuman. Sexual decoration.

Feel the sadness of living in a world like this.

If you are capable, and even if you aren't sure you are, feel the sadness of being a part of the group of people that has most violently and repeatedly created and maintained a world like this. Feel the excruciating pain of complicity.

Don't soothe it with thoughts of your own exceptionalism. Don't jump to demonstrate your love of women. Don't talk about your mother or your sister or daughter. Just sit. Feel the feelings.

You honor the pain that has been expressed so courageously by giving yourself over to the discomfort of actually feeling what it is to live in this world—a world filled with sexual harassment and assault—as a man. Sitting with that discomfort will change you. And the changed you can then take action with a different kind of wisdom.

I'm asking you to do this because it is similar to the discomfort and wiser action I am striving for with regard to my whiteness. In other words, I know it isn't easy. I'm trying to do this myself—trying to actually feel the grief and unpack the privileges that produce surprise in me when a group of white supremacists takes to the streets in Charlottesville in 2017. I want nothing to do with them, but they are part of me. We share the same skin color. We share a country. We share a horrifying and unhealed history.

So you, my guy friend—if you are moved by the courage of the testimony you are reading, you must dig in and meet that courage with stillness and softness. Don't be good or right. Don't distance yourself from the possibility of violation and violence. Move closer to your own confusion and earnest desire to understand the sickness at the center of contemporary masculinity, a bit of which, *at least* a bit of which, you, too, are suffering from.

Reflect on how it might be showing up in your home, in your workplace, in your school. Not just as harassment or assault—as arrogance, as obliviousness, as narcissism, as domination. Consider journaling. Consider reading. Consider therapy. If you think you've figured it out, if you are tempted to explain it, start over. Get really, really humble. This is going to take a long time. A lifetime. Learn how to notice your emotions before you fling them out into the world in some other form. Reclaim the child you were before they told you how to be a man. Remember his tenderness, his curiosity, his wholeness. Realize that your liberation is tied up in ours.

Then, and only then, gather with other men and have incredibly awkward conversations about the feelings that are arising in this moment, in these explorations. Model what it looks like to say hard things in front of other dudes. Be earnest even when you'd rather make a joke. Don't get trashed while you do it. Try to stay sober and look other guys in the eye. Teach each other how to call other men out when they are belittling and overlooking and harassing and abusing women (and other men).

Don't do this for your daughters and wives and mothers. Do this for your sons. Do this for yourselves. Don't use an apologetic tone in a women's studies class; use an unapologetic tone at the bus stop or at your book club or around the Thanksgiving dinner table, or yes, on Facebook. Take it personally, together. Consider it urgent, together. One of the delusions that privileged people often have is that we can fix things, efficiently and alone. Know this: you cannot fix this. The journey will not be efficient. You cannot go it alone.

A world this riddled with sexual harassment and abuse will never be healed by a hashtag, that's for sure.

Yet this moment could be the first one in which you choose to do something different, to lay the first brick in a world that is built differently, a world safe for women's bodies and men's feelings, a world worthy of everyone's wholeness.

Courtney E. Martin is a columnist for *On Being*. Her column appears every Friday.
Her newest book, *The New Better Off: Reinventing the American Dream*, explores how people are redefining the American dream (think more fulfillment, community, and fun, less debt, status, and stuff). Courtney is the co-founder of the Solutions Journalism Network and a strategist for the TED Prize. She is also co-founder and partner at Valenti Martin Media and FRESH Speakers Bureau, and editor emeritus at Feministing.com.
Courtney has authored/edited five books, including *Do It Anyway: The New Generation of Activists*, and *Perfect Girls, Starving Daughters: How the Quest for Perfection is Harming Young Women*. Her work appears frequently in *The New York Times* and *The Washington Post*. Courtney has appeared on the TODAY Show, Good Morning America, MSNBC, and The O'Reilly Factor, and speaks widely at conferences and colleges. She is the recipient of the Elie Wiesel Prize in Ethics and a residency from the Rockefeller Foundation's Bellagio Centre. She lives with her partner in life and work, John Cary, in Oakland, and their daughters Maya and Stella. Read more about her work at www.courtneyemartin.com.

The Wild Feminine Freed #MeToo
By Jamie Della

When you embrace your fiercest, most joyful, most uninhibited freedom, the Wild Feminine cackles and howls in delight, piercing the bubble of shame and releasing its grip on you.

I held up the pink hibiscus to the wind and laughed a seven-year-old giggle, delighted at the orange pollen that was released into the air. My 11-year-old neighbor smiled at my glee and passed me a note. "Do you want to have sex? Check the box, Yes or No." I didn't know what sex was, but I said yes, just to be daring. I asked my younger sister go into the bathroom with us. We were all naked, the tile floor was cold and hard, he had a band-aid on his butt. But my sister's look of horror frightened me most. Until the babysitter knocked on the door and in my haste, I put on my top inside out.

Shame haunts the sexually assaulted and keeps us locked away in the recesses of our brains, on the outskirts of a "pure" society, trapped in an all-consuming belief of our unworthiness. We become the outcasts. Our silence is our jail keeper.

If only we remembered that the key to freedom hides in our womb.

We must claim our sovereignty by owning the power of the pussy.

Our liberation awaits when we draw out the lusty Baba Yaga: the Goddess who dares us to go boldly in the direction of our bliss, face our fears and liberate our shame. Baba Yaga indulges in our warrior, wanton ways and every life-giving "yes" we utter. And for our hard work, this Goddess grants us a powerful light in a naked skull to light our way and incinerate those forces that do not serve our highest good.

I enjoyed and feared sex as a young woman. But I had no idea how to flirt without it turning into being dominated or raped. I counted the notches in the bedpost with pride and shame. The word "slut" raced through my head during sex and I would curl up in a fetal position, riddled with a merciless shame that I was a horrible, despicable person. Years later, I decided I had enough pain. Stopped it dead in its tracks and swung the pendulum far into sexual freedom and multiple orgasms.

We need to bond together in Sacred Sisterhood with Baba Yaga, the Bone Mother, at our helm.

Don't wait for the next demonstration to wear your pink pussy hat: wear it skiing on the slopes this winter. Let us wear that pentacle or goddess pendant or gold cross proudly and never condemn another sister for her choice in how she sees the Divine. Let us reclaim our right to sacred birth and sacred death with midwives and doulas, singing, drumming, stories. Let us never be ashamed of our menses: it is the most sacred ritual for it is the Ceremony of Life, every single moon. Let us have our cycle for a time of rest, reflection and rejuvenation: the powers of the Wild Feminine.

Follow your intuition—the nudgings of the Goddess showing the way to your Personal North. Each time you follow your inner voice, your intuition becomes stronger, like a muscle that grows with use.

For the times you are too afraid to listen, never let shame overwhelm you. Create an altar where you can remember the Goddess that lives in you, as you.

And always remember that the Divine lives in the Mundane and the Mundane in the Divine as fallible, holy **you**.

Baba Yaga can free me by standing beside me through all my challenges, demanding me to rise again and again. I rode on her broom of mortar and pestle until I could allow the wind to blow through my hair in unapologetic wild abandon and not fear that it would inadvertently elicit desire in another. I knew how to protect myself with Bone Mother at my side.

Jamie Della is the author of eight books on the Divine Feminine and Latina culture (published as Jamie Wood). She is a storyteller, teacher, potter, and healer in the Eastern Sierra Mountains where she hosts travelers from all walks of life with warmth, kindness and the power of the Divine Feminine.

Our Bodies Are Not the Problem
By Liz DeBetta

Rebecca Solnit, in a recent article in The Guardian, said, *"Being unable to tell your story is a living death, and sometimes a literal one... Stories save your life. And are your life. We are our stories; stories that can be both prison and the crowbar to break open the door of that prison."*

In the past 24 hours I have read a story about sexism as a political force, a story about the misogyny enabled by digital communication platforms, watched a video that asks what's more offensive than little girls saying fuck?, and a video of Daniel Craig in drag, to elucidate the complete lack of any kind of gender equality as a result of rampant sexism, misogyny and resulting violence to women and girls across the United States and the world. This is nothing new. There are countless stories like these strewn across various media platforms every day. So much so that some may argue that it diminishes the importance of these stories. I beg to differ. The problem is not how many stories there are, but the fact that no one is paying attention. No one is giving them proper credence.

The stories are being diminished because they are being told by women. They are women's stories. They are the words that give voice to the violence, the oppression, the indignity of being treated like an object. Like an other. Like a piece of meat. Or property. Or only valued because you're hot. Or not valued because you're fat. Or ignored because you're trans. Or black. Or brown. Or mixed. Or indefinable.

They placed a statue of a little girl defiantly confronting the bull on Wall Street. Why not a woman? Because a little girl is cute and manageable and palatable to the kind of watered down feminism that many people seem willing to placate. Some can be advocates as long as it's not too offensive, as long as it doesn't offend their husbands, fathers, ministers or precious children. Some can be advocates as long as it means they are still being demure and acceptable. As long as it doesn't make anyone uncomfortable. But that's bullshit. It is uncomfortable. It needs to be uncomfortable if we are ever going to see any progress. As a woman I am uncomfortable. And I will not continue to be silenced.

I woke up dancing with ghosts -
Mine, yours, hers, theirs
Haunted by the history of hurt
Hurtling through the hell of remembering
Exorcism is not easy

Our bodies are not the problem

It's boys that are too scared they're "not man enough"
Manning up to some ideal that always being in control

is necessary
Never let them see you cry
Emotion is weakness and we'll save that shit for them

Pussies

Pound down the pain
Pretend it's not there
Take it out on her, them, me

In the dark

Behind a dumpster

Locked in a stall

In someone's basement

In my apartment

Debase us in favor of feeling the truth
Assault us like we are the salt in your festering wound
Wound so tight

Our bodies are not the problem

It's being told to be pure
To wait until marriage
To not give away the milk before the cow
To wait
To be The Madonna and not The Whore
There is no happy medium
You are either too much or not enough

Lori Perkins

But still you are the target
Of so much rage

So much shame

So much unadulterated fear

Our bodies are not the problem

10/20/2017

Liz DeBetta holds an MA in English from the City University of New York - College of Staten Island, a BA in Theater/Speech from Wagner College, and is pursuing a PhD in Interdisciplinary Studies with an emphasis in Women's and Gender Studies at Union Institute & University. She is currently a Lecturer in the First Year Writing Program at Utah Valley University, and the writing and performance mentor for *Act Risk No More,* a non-profit theater group whose mission is to write and perform poetry and prose to create socially conscious theater that tells the stories of each group member, and sheds light on issues like depression, anxiety, domestic violence, sexual identity, inclusion, loneliness, anger, and abuse. The stories told are of survival and hope. They remind us that no one is alone, and that the voicing of stories can save lives. She is a member of Actor's Equity and SAG-AFTRA, and is interested in writing for healing and social change from a feminist perspective. www.lizdebetta.com

Hush

By Sherri Donovan

It happened at the tailor
In the corner of the room
Chubby fingers gliding over her red sweatered breasts
He said he needed to check for more buttons on her
coat;

It happened at the lawyer's office
His words so elegant
As a tool of distraction
To accomplish his real aim
Moving magician's hands on her thighs;

It happened at the doctor's office
pressing so hard inside her to check
for virginity;

It happened in his own bed
His uncle locking the door
Pulling out his dagger

Quick dirty secrets
Makes her want to scream and shower

1000 times and whack them in their groins
Publish their names on billboards as molesters

Alas, Surreal hush
No acknowledgement
Busy life uninterrupted
As if it never happened.

Sherri Donovan is a published author, blogger and family lawyer. Sherri has published a book of poetry, *Matryoshka Rising: Poetic Briefs* in 2016, available on Amazon, and a nonfiction book on divorce in 2005. Her poems have also been published in *The Poetry Table Anthology, 2016.* Sherri has performed her poems at the Cornelia Café, New York County Lawyers Association, and in salons, poetry circles and festivals.

Ms. Donovan has had articles published in *The Huffington Post, New York Law Journal, Cosmopolitan* and *Parent* magazines. She has also spoken before the United Nations and various bar associations.

Sexual Harassment on the Job from HR's Perspective

By Marina Jumiga

I asked someone who works in HR to give us an insider's view of what goes through their minds when there's a violation at work, and how these issues are handled. Not everyone works for a conglomerate or glitzy entertainment business, but everyone—be they a teacher, nurse, cashier—should talk to HR when they experience a violation. Marina Jumiga works in the Healthcare field. - Lori Perkins, Editor

It's change of shift, and I'm running through the halls as usual, because there's just never enough time in the day to accomplish what's on my to-do list. It's something that kind of keeps me on track for a minute, until something else that is much more important interrupts my flow. At this time of day there is a line of those clocking out after working the morning shift, and those who are impatiently waiting to clock in, because no one wants to be docked for being late. There is a lot of "hellos," "good-byes," "how you doin's," and "haven't seen you in a while's"—and then, suddenly, there's a tap on the butt. I see it, I hear it and I'm furious.

Did we just replace a handshake?! Everyone in favor, please say "aye."

* * *

The conference room is quiet and it feels empty, even though it is completely packed with employees of all job titles, ranging from "Certified Nursing Assistant" to "Director," as we have yet another meeting on behavior in the workplace.

I address the room: "If you see something, or if you experience something inappropriate, I urge you to say something," I tell them. "That is the reason why we have this training: it's important to know that sexual harassment is unacceptable in the workplace. It's dangerous and can lead to poor work performance, depression, increased absenteeism, and, eventually, resignation. To prevent this from happening, Human Resources (HR) needs to be told, so that they can do their work and fix it. The employee handbook that is given to every new hire at our Nursing Home and Rehabilitation Center clearly states that 'sexual harassment in the workplace will not be tolerated, and is a terminable offense.' It is not a joke, and it's not funny. It's vital that staff knows where to go to seek advice, help and resolution for an action/remark/look/touch that is inappropriate and uncomfortable for them."

"According to the Bureau of Labor Statistics," I say, "a person spends on average 8.8 hours a day at work. That is enough time to do your work and to make friends. It's enough time to get to know your co-workers and their habits, likes and dislikes. Unfortunately, for some, it's also enough time to get so comfortable that they forget they are at work, where professionalism and a sense of distance should always remain intact."

Now that I've acknowledged the elephant in the room, I ask, "Will anyone step up and tell me that they are feeling scared, or helpless, or nervous to work on the fourth floor? Or do you get nauseous just thinking about the sexual assault you've experienced while working on the night shift? This is what the Human Resources office is for: you, the employees," I remind them. "We are here to answer your questions, to solve your problems, to comfort you and guide you," I say. "We don't judge, we don't disclose, and we don't let go until you're ready."

I continue. "Don't rely on cameras," I warn, "they are good but tricky. Suppose you are in the staircase, or walk into the bathroom with a few stalls, or suppose you are in a resident's/patient's room." Everyone knows that would be a HIPPA violation. "Medication or stockrooms are also places where cameras are not installed; where you could be a victim of a sexual assault. If you don't tell HR that this has happened to you, we won't know. I can't help you if you don't tell me."

I explain the procedure: "Let me share with you what happens once you let HR know of an incident. First, a complete investigation will be conducted. The company's sexual harassment policy will be explained to you, and you will be informed how the investigation will run. Then complainants and the respondents' statements will be collected and witnesses will be interviewed. Once that is complete, an informal means of resolving the alleged harassment will be explored.

For example, the two persons involved would no longer be working on the same unit and/or shift. If warranted, the allegation will be reported to the police, and if the assault is substantiated, the respondent will be terminated. HR will prepare a written report for the employee files, and will set up a meeting with management in an effort to come up with ideas for preventing—no, scratch that…stopping—sexual harassment and assault from happening in the future."

As I sit here writing this with my cup of tea and a fortune cookie in front of me, the piece of paper sticking out from one of the halves reads, "change your thoughts and you can change the world."

I've done everything in my power as an HR person to do what I must do to help in this sexual harassment case. I assure you that this employee will never use a tap on the butt as a hello statement ever again: not in this facility or in any other. This incident prompted numerous other actions that I, as HR, was able to come up with. The conclusion of this incident was that the abuser was reprimanded and terminated, and I subsequently had the educator conduct an in-service training throughout the whole facility, with a sign-in sheet to establish that everyone had attended. That way, no one would be able to give an excuse of not knowing the policy on sexual harassment. They are all now well aware that such behavior is not welcomed, and will not be tolerated in this facility under my watch.

Sexual harassment cases are the hardest in the HR profession; at least for me they are, but they are also the most rewarding. Everyone should have the freedom to move around the facility without worrying about being touched or being spoken to inappropriately. It's never easy to let someone go for something that could have been avoided, but in my facility, we say hello with words and a smile.

Marina Jumiga is a Human Resources Assistant at Atrium Center for Rehab and Nursing in Brooklyn, NY. She graduated summa cum laude with a Master's degree in Industrial and Organizational Psychology, and magna cum laude with a Bachelor's in Forensic Psychology and a minor in Gender Studies from John Jay College of Criminal Justice. She is mother to two beautiful girls and a wife to the most amazing husband ever. In her "spare time" she drinks tea, watches Netflix and attempts to clean the kitchen.

Why the #MeToo Movement is a Call to Arms for Men Everywhere
By Mark Radcliffe
(Originally published by the Good Men Project)

Like many men today, I watched with a mix of sorrow, disbelief, rage and even a vague sense of complicity as each new "#MeToo" post filled up my Facebook feed.

"Dear God," I thought. "Not her, too."

Again.

And again.

And again.

And again.

By day's end it seemed pretty clear: there might not be a single woman in my life who hasn't dealt with sexual assault at one point or another. Given the sheer numbers I saw, and the likelihood that many more are still in the shadows and not quite ready to declare it publicly, if you're a woman, and you've been around long enough, you've probably been groped, touched, kissed, or far worse by a man without your consent. By your boss, a "friend," a colleague, a stranger in a bar, or even a cab driver.

We men have heard the stats before, that "one in five women has been raped," and found it already too devastating to believe, but after today, with the sheer unanimity of women who have experienced something traumatizing at the hands of men, the terrifying scope of it is far too visible for us to ignore.

So the lesson for us men is simple:

This is a problem that men have caused.

So we can't expect women to fix it all on their own, even as brave and helpful as these posts are.

And it's not enough for us men to just *not* assault women.

We have to do more. Not just *not be part of the problem*, but actively be part of the solution.

Because if this is a daily reality for all women, it hurts us, too. As their boyfriends, husbands, brothers, sons, friends and, hell, even just by virtue of standing here on the same planet with them. If their days are filled with dread/fear/anxiety/depression, then their lives are forever worsened. And we share those lives with them—if one part suffers, every part suffers with it. As a result, women are understandably less open with us, less trusting of us, and less able to be fully alive and present in our lives as well. And this simply cannot be.

So what are we actively doing to help prevent it? Or what are we doing to at least help women who've been victimized to achieve justice? Because, as Edmund Burke once wrote, "All that is necessary for the triumph of evil is that good men do nothing."

So to all "good" men out there: We must do more. Much more.

How?

We can start by simply being the kind of supportive friend/boyfriend/husband/ colleague that a woman feels comfortable discussing her assault with. By being someone who genuinely cares about others, who asks about how others are doing, who can genuinely sense when someone shows up at work the next day and clearly isn't quite themselves, and by saying, "Hey, you seem a little down today. Is something going on? If you want to talk, let me know, we'll go somewhere quiet and I'll be all ears." Because I keep thinking about times when I could have made a difference, and I'm saying to myself, "I wish she'd known she could have trusted me with that. Maybe I could have helped." But I only found out today. Long after the damage was done.

Maybe that conversation entails us just being a pair of ears and a source of support. Maybe it involves us getting involved, and being willing to help her confront the person, approach HR, or even go with her to the police. And that might be really hard. But it's necessary.

This is just the beginning.

The real challenge is in going to be working on our fellow men. Every. Single. Day.

Being an agent of change in the daily conversations we're a part of. When an entire conversation with "the boys" at a restaurant is about the waitress' ass, what are we doing to change that?

When your buddy is "swiping right" on 200 Tinder profiles in a row and copying and pasting "DTF?", are you willing to get into it with him? Say, "Dude, is this the kind of guy you want to be in the world?"

Helping warn our female friends when they're interested in a particularly charming guy and we've heard that their charm is only used to disarm women before taking advantage of them?

Watching for when the guys we're out on the town with are crossing a line with a woman. Maybe being nearby in case things get out of control, a guy is making unwanted advances and a woman needs another man there to intercede. And yes, being willing to have that guy hate us for it.

Playing brother's keeper: "Look dude, Laura told me about what happened when you walked her home last night. Maybe you were drunk, maybe you think it was consensual, but dude, it wasn't. You have to apologize to her and try to make things right, and never do it again. If you don't, well, sorry, but I can't be friends with you anymore. And I'll let my female friends know that this is how you roll."

And then the ultimate challenge: when some guy you work with—or even work for—has crossed a line with someone, are you willing to take her side instead of his? Even if it hurts your career? Yes, going to HR with her and saying you saw him inappropriately groping her at the company party and be willing to face the backlash? Yes, even if HR dismisses it and decides to take the boss' side and fires you for insubordination? If you are, then you/me/we are finally, truly being part of the solution.

We might have to get another job, we might have to have some uncomfortable conversations with our fellow men, we might have to unfriend them, tell them we can't hang out anymore, we might even have to be willing to come to blows with some prick in a bar who won't take a woman's "no" for an answer.

But we have to make these men face more consequences than they currently are.

Because if their moral compass won't compel

them to act differently, then we must make the consequences of their actions force them to change—both in their behavior and attitudes.

And if we do that, we will no longer be fully complicit in a world that results in umpteen million women having to post "#MeToo" in their Facebook feed today.

So gentlemen, let's pledge to have a lot more difficult conversations between ourselves, so that there are fewer difficult "#MeToo" posts from the women in our lives.

Mark Radcliffe is a writer living in New York City. He has a weakness for bourbon, jazz and women who can drive stick. You can read more of his essays here: www.theradcliffescrolls.tumblr.com and http://markradcliffe.com.

Politics is My #MeToo
By Alessandra Biaggi

When I was five years old I recall walking into our high-rise building one afternoon, past a room full of people voting. Unclear why they had gathered, I asked, "What are they doing?" to which my parents replied, "voting for their leaders. I immediately told my parents, "I want to be a leader."

A few short years later, I recall telling my parents that I aspired to run for office. Not really grasping the magnitude of what a public servant is required to absorb or provide, I wanted to emulate the work that my grandfather, Congressman Mario Biaggi (D-NY) was doing. He cared very deeply about his constituents, and the community, and dedicated his life's work to making life better for others. It should come as no surprise, then, that it was encouraged, rather than taboo, to speak politics at the dinner table, and it's where I learned how to negotiate and support my views about policies and current events. I have my deeply thoughtful and caring parents to thank for that.

After the 2016 election that ambition only grew stronger, and for the first time I started "getting to work" by putting my thoughts and plans on paper.

Prior to working at Hillary for America, my strong interest and faith in empowering women through legal and political processes led me to attend the Women's Campaign School at Yale University, and later to participate in additional campaign trainings, offered by Progressive and Pro-Democratic organizations such as the New Leaders Council and Eleanor's Legacy, and the non-partisan organization championing women in politics, SheShouldRun.

The combination of knowledge I acquired from these trainings, accompanied by the burning fire to *act*, which I felt from our devastating loss, left me frustrated and hopeless. But through days (and nights) of crying and meditation—it finally came to me: a tenet of mindfulness that has driven me during times of utter desperation and failure. The principle goes something like this:

In times when you feel like you need love, give love. When you feel alone and need community, gather people in togetherness. When you feel a lack of resources, start from where you are, with what you have, and create.

And, little by little—I began to do just that. I knew that if I didn't get out of bed and into the arena I'd be missing an opportunity to participate in one of the most historically political times of need ever witnessed by our great nation. I kept my shortcomings in mind, but I was also keenly aware of what I actually possessed as an offering. I had a law degree, a strong knowledge of civics, I was a woman who worked in politics seeing the challenges women often faced, and the points of entry into the political beast of campaigns and governing. There were many angles to present this information, but for the first time ever in my life, I didn't over think it; I just opened a Google Word document and started writing, because in my moments of deep sadness and despair, I knew that the only way I would rise out of bed in the morning and start to heal was to begin sharing this part of myself.

Focused on igniting women and millennials to get off the sidelines and into political office, especially in the nascent months of our loss, I was inspired to create the rituals of mindful democracy through civic engagement in the *Take Action Guide for Activism.* This comprehensive guide was inspired by Alexis de Tocqueville's *Rituals of Democracy in America,* and it became a reference text for organizations, research, protests and communities, and for anyone who wanted to get involved and make a change. It was created for any and all levels of experience, as a chance to participate in politics no matter what one's interest, unmet need or strength. Want to take campaign training? There's something in there for you. Need a thorough, thoughtful and honest read about the current state of racism, sexism and misogyny in the US? Articles fill the pages. The list is endless and collaborative—its growth only made possible through my first step—sharing my resources— and through my second step of connecting with others and adding the zeitgeist into it.

The result—after taking a leap of faith that anyone would even care to read this document—was a shock: I received the great privilege of invitations to speak at many public and at private events on topics including women in politics, leadership, civics, political strategy, and community organizing for Ladies Get Paid, Rally + Rise, New York University's Women's Initiative, Impact

Hub, Solidarity Sundays, Columbia University, Changemaker Chats, theAll In Together Campaign, The Arena, Breakout Today with Diane Von Furstenberg, and the latest with New York's Lieutenant Governor, Kathleen C. Hochul. It also lead to getting the word out, and sharing this information with all of you, who will then go on to share it with others.

Sure, politics can be a dirty experience, and sometimes I want to throw in the towel for good. But most days I remember how the power of community, connection and storytelling can literally set us free. The dirty part? That neither scares me, nor makes me question whether this is my path. Politics represents, for me, the most meaningful work, the most exciting journey worth the challenging adventure, and, most importantly, an avenue where you can do the most good, and have the most impact in the short time we have on this earth.

In the messiness of what politics often unearths, I prioritize truth telling even over safety, comfort, or fear. I am proud, but even more humbled by what we women have accomplished together since November 8, 2016. How we have risen en masse. How we have used our voices to topple oppressive patriarchal power.

But we are just beginning. The road is long, and we will grow weary, but we must never give up or give in. I am honored to join the stories of my sisters; together our voices will reverberate—throughout the streets, rounding corners that echo through the halls of Congress and state legislatures; that rip through industries, which have historically protected predators and upheld systems of abuse. Enough. Our message— spoken + written - is united. #MeToo.

Alessandra Biaggi worked on the New York staff of the Hilary for America Campaign in 2016. She holds a legal degree from Fordham University, has studied at Yale University in the Women's Campaign League, and is the granddaughter of New York Congressman Mario Biaggi.

About the Editor

Lori Perkins is a published author, book editor and literary agent with three decades experience in publishing newspapers and books. She was the owner and publisher of the Uptown Weekly News in Manhattan's Washington Heights and Inwood in the 80's, as well as an adjunct professor of journalism at NYU. She has written or edited 30 books, 25 of which have been erotic romance anthologies. She was the editor of the very first zombie romance anthology, *Hungry for Your Love*, and the editor of the nonfiction collection of essays *50 Writers on 50 Shades of Grey*, as well as *1984 in the 21st Century* and is the co-author of *Everything You Always Wanted to Know About Watergate (But Were Afraid to Ask)*. She is the founder of the L. Perkins Agency, an established New York literary agency with numerous books on the New York Times bestseller list, as well as the Publisher of Riverdale Avenue Books, an award-winning hybrid publisher. She is currently working on a series of naughty historicals with USA Today bestselling author Jamie Schmidt under the nom de plume Lorna James. You can follow her on Twitter at @LoriPerkinsRAB.

Other Riverdale Avenue Books You Might Enjoy

1984 in the 21st Century: An Anthology of Essays
Edited by Lori Perkins

Everything You Always Wanted to Know about Watergate
(But Were Afraid to Ask)
By Brian J. O'Connor and Lori Perkins

Flashes: Adventures in Dating Through Menopause
By Michelle Churchill

Smoke, Drink F*#k
By Christine Dodd

Confessions of a Librarian
By Barbara Foster

Physical Ed: Book One of the Sex University Series
By Louisa Bacio

Escaped: Book One of the Running in Fear Series
By Trinity Blacio

The Ripper Letter: Book One in the Hearts of Darkness Series
By Katherine Ramsland

The Morris-Jumel Mansion Anthology of Fantasy and Paranormal Fiction
Edited by Camilla Saly-Monzingo

Made in the USA
Middletown, DE
17 January 2020